Discovering Biblical Treasures

UNDERSTANDING: EZRA

A commentary using Ancient Bible Study Methods

Michael Harvey Koplitz

ACKNOWLEDGMENTS

This work could not have been accomplished without Dr. Anne Davis, who taught me the Ancient Bible (Hebraic) study methods, and my two study partners, Rev. Dr. Robert Cook and Pastor Sandra Koplitz. We know that the journey has just started and will last a lifetime. The discovery of the depths of God's Word is waiting for us to find.

4

Table of Contents

INTRODUCTION

After 2000 years of Christian theology and thought, the original meaning to the Scriptures, especially the Christian Scriptures, has come to us today with a vast number of filters. These filters include the theological interpretations that have developed over the years about the meaning of the Scriptures. Unfortunately, Christianity divorced itself from its mother religion, Judaism, by the end of the first century C.E. By doing so, combined with the dwindling number of Jews in the church, the Hebraic understanding of the Scriptures was mostly lost and eventually considered invalid by the church Bishops. Ignatius of Antioch (died in 107 C.E.) in his Epistle to the Magnesians wrote, "To profess Jesus Christ while continuing to follow Jewish customs is an absurdity. The Christian faith does not look to Judaism, but Judaism looks to Christianity."[1]

In addition to the filters, there is much cultural information not contained in the narratives of the Scriptures because the people of the Bible knew their own culture. A modern example is this. If you were to write in your diary you went to church on Sunday; there would be a lot of information you would not include. Anyone reading your diary entry would know certain things intuitively. Some of these things would be (1) You drove your car; (2) The car had gasoline in it; (3) You had a driver's license; (4) You had paid for car insurance, to list a few items. The same applies when the narratives of the Scriptures are read. When a narrative says that Yeshua's disciples went into a field and picked grain, the narrator does not have to explain how grain was picked and how it was prepared for consumption.

---

[1] Friedman, David. *They Loved the Torah: What Yeshua's First Followers Really Thought about the Law*. Baltimore, MD: Lederer Books, 2001.

Another example would be the marriage story. The original listeners of the Scriptures did not need an explanation of what happened at a Jewish wedding. Read the account of Yeshua at the wedding at Cana, and you will find there is much cultural information left out about the ceremony and celebration because the people knew it of the day.

So, to obtain a complete understanding of the Scriptures, especially the words of Yeshua, we need to learn how to think as a person did in Yeshua's days. This can be done by combining the culture and customs of the people with a linguistic approach of the Scriptures. The people "listened" intently for the linguistic clues that led to a depth of meaning because they did not have books or copies of the Scriptures to read. The Scriptures were passed down through the generations by a mouth to ear method.

Much has been written about the customs and manners of the ancient world; therefore, current research is sufficient. What makes this dissertation unique is that it is the combination of culture and to offer a Hebraic understanding of Scripture from Yeshua's day as the Jewish listener heard it.

Dr. Robert Price makes an argument in his article <u>New Testament Narrative as Old Testament Midrash</u> that the New Testament is a retelling of the Old Testament, thus creating aggadah.[2] "The New Testament gospels and the Acts of the Apostles can be shown to be Christian aggadah upon Jewish scripture, and these narratives can be

---

[2] Aggadah is "the non legal or narrative material, as parables, maxims, or anecdotes, in the Talmud and other rabbinical literature, serving either to illustrate the meaning or purpose of the law, custom, or Biblical passage being discussed or to introduce a different, unrelated topic." Source: "The Definition of Aggadah." *Dictionary.com*. N.p., n.d. Web. 1 Aug. 2016.

neither fully understood nor fully appreciated without tracing them to their underlying sources, the object of the present article."[3]

What is the Greek system of learning? J. Parsons expresses an overview of this system of learning in his article <u>Theology and the Greek Mindset</u>. "The modern university, for example, was modeled after the ideals of Plato's Academy in which (it was hoped) the entire universe would be explained within its halls."[4] Today's Seminaries and Bible Colleges are part of the modern university system and therefore, are using the learning methodology that Plato and his contemporaries used to view the universe. This system of learning and understanding is a part of our current education system. Therefore, when teachers, who are considered experts in their field of study, instruct students, it is often frowned upon for the student to challenge the teacher or to create a debate when the student might not agree with the teacher's interpretation. Besides, the Greek method of learning calls the study of Scripture hermeneutics. Hermeneutics is "the science of interpretation, especially of the Scriptures."[5] This Greek approach is very different from the Hebraic method proposed by this study.

The learning methods of Socrates and his contemporaries make sense when studying, for example, "The Iliad" by Homer or other Greek philosophic documents, but these methods do not necessarily bring to life all of the flavors of ancient Middle Eastern documents. This Greek approach is the method of Bible study that has been employed by Christianity for over 1900 years.

---

[3] Price, Robert M. "New Testament Narrative as Old Testament Midrash." In *The Christ-myth Theory and Its Problems*, 1. Cranford, NJ: American Atheist Press, 2011. Accessed August 01, 2016. http://www.robertmprice.mindvendor.com/art_midrash1.htm.

[4] Parsons, John. "Theology and the Greek Mindset - a Brief Look." Theology and the Greek Mindset - a Brief Look. Accessed August 01, 2016. http://www.hebrew4christians.com/Articles/Hellenism/hellenism.html.

[5] "Hermeneutics." Dictionary.com. Accessed April 14, 2016. http://dictionary.reference.com/browse/hermeneutics.

Ezra's book is a postexilic book meaning that it was written toward the end of the seventy-year Exile the Hebrew people faced after their destruction by Babylon. Ezra was born in Babylon and educated there. His role was in the restoration of the remnant of Israel who returned to Judea and Jerusalem. It is believed that this book was written in Aramaic because that was the imperial language of the Persian and Babylonian Empires. It was transcribed into Hebrew later on. Some parts of the book are in Aramaic. The book was probably written in the fourth century BCE.

THE MAIN DIFFERENCES BETWEEN THE GREEK METHOD AND THE HEBRAIC METHOD OF TEACHING

Once a student becomes aware of these two teaching styles, the student will be able to determine if the class attended or if a book was read, whether the teaching method is either a Greek or Hebraic method. In the Greek manner, the instructor is always right because of advanced knowledge. In the college situation, it is because the professor has his/her Ph.D. in some area of study, so one assumes that he or she knows everything about the topic. For example, Rodney Dangerfield played the role of a middle-aged man going to college. His English midterm was to write about Kurt Vonnegut Jr. Since he did not understand any of Vonnegut's books, he hired Vonnegut himself to write the midterm. When he received the paper from the English professor told Dangerfield that whoever wrote the paper knew nothing about Vonnegut. The professor's words are an example of the Greek method of teaching. Did the PhD English professor think that she knew more about Vonnegut's writings than Vonnegut did? [6]

In the Greek teaching method, the professor or the instructor claims to be the authority. If one attends a Bible study class and the class leader says, "I will teach you the only way to understand this biblical book," you may want to consider the implications. This method is standard since most Seminaries and Bible colleges teach a Greek mode of learning, which is the same method the church has been utilizing for centuries.

Hebraic teaching methods are different. The teacher wants the students to challenge what they hear. It is through questioning that a student can learn. Also, the teacher wants his/her students to excel to a point where the student becomes the teacher.

---

[6] *Back to School*. Performed by Rodney Dangerfield. Hollywood: CA: Paper Clip Productions, 1986. DVD.

If two rabbis come together to discuss a passage of Scripture, the result will be at least ten different opinions. All points of view are acceptable if each is supported by biblical evidence. It is permissible and encouraged that students develop many ideas. There is a depth to God's Word, and God wants us to find all His messages contained in the Scripture.

Seeking out the meaning of the Scriptures beyond the literal meaning is essential to fully understand God's Word.[7] The Greek method of learning the Scriptures has prevailed over the centuries. One problem is that only the literal interpretation of Scripture was often viewed as valid, as prompted by Martin Luther's "sola literalis," meaning that just the literal translation of Scripture was accurate. The Fundamentalist movements of today base their beliefs on the literal interpretation of the Scripture. Therefore, they do not believe that God placed more profound, hidden, or secret meanings in the Word.

The students of the Scriptures who learn through Hebraic training and understanding have drawn a different conclusion. The Hebrew language itself leads to different possible interpretations because of the construction of the language. The Hebraic method of Bible study opens avenues of thought about God's revelations in the Scripture never considered. Not all questions about the Scripture studied will have an immediate answer. If so, it becomes the responsibility of the learners to uncover the meaning. Also, remember that many opinions about the meaning of Scripture are also acceptable.

---

[7] Davis, Anne Kimball. *The Synoptic Gospels*. MP3. Albuquerque: NM: BibleInteract, 2012.

METHODOLOGY

The methodology employed is to use First Century Scripture study methods integrated with Yeshua's customs and culture to examine the Hebrew and Christian Scriptures, thus gathering a more in-depth understanding by learning the Scriptures in the way the people of Yeshua's day did.

I have titled the methodology of analyzing a passage of Scripture in a Hebraic manner the "Process of Discovery." The author developed this methodology, which brings together various areas of linguistic and cultural understanding. There are several sections to the process, and not all the parts apply to every passage of Scripture. The overall result of developing this process is to give the reader a framework for studying the word in more depth.

The "Process of Discovery" starts with a Scripture passage. An examination of the linguistic structure of the passage is next. The linguistic structure includes parallelism, chiastic structures, and repetition. Formatting the passage in its linguistic form allows the reader to be able to visualize what the first century CE listener was hearing. Their corresponding sections label the chiasms, for example, A, B, C, B', A.' Not all passages of the Scriptures have a poetic form.

The next step is to "question the narrative." The questioning the narrative process assuming the reader knows nothing about the passage. Therefore, the questions go from the simple to the complex. The next task is to identify any linguistic patterns. Linguistic patterns include, but are not limited to, irony, simile, metaphor, symbolism, idioms, hyperbole, figurative language, personification, and allegory.

A review of any translation inconsistencies discovered between the English NAU version and either the Hebrew or Greek versions is done. There are times when a Hebrew or Greek word is translated in more than one way. Inconsistencies also can be created by the translation committee, which may have decided to use traditional language instead of the actual translation. The decision of the translation committee is in the Preface or Introduction to the Bible. Perhaps some of the inconsistencies were intentionally added to convey some deeper meaning. An examination for every discrepancy is done.

The passage is analyzed for any echoes of the Hebrew Scriptures in the Christian Scriptures. Using a passage from the Hebrew Scriptures in the Christian Scriptures, an echo occurs.[8] Also, echoes are found when Torah (Genesis through Deuteronomy) passages are used in other Hebrew Bible books. Cross-references in the Scripture are references from one verse to another verse which can assist the reader in understanding the verse.

The names of persons mentioned in the passage are listed. Many of the Hebrew names have meaning and may be associated with places or actions. Jewish parents used to name their children based on what they felt God had in store for their child. An example of this is Abraham, whose original name was Abram and was changed to mean eternal father (God changed Abram's name to Abraham, indicating a function he was to perform). When the Hebrew Bible gives names, many of the occurrences mean something unique. The same importance can occur for the names of places. The time it takes to travel between locations can supply insight into the event.

---

[8] Mitzvot are the 613 commandments found in the Torah that please God. There are positive and negative commandments. The list was first development by Maimonides. The full list can be found at: ttp://www.jewfaq.org/613.htm.

Keyphrases are identified in verses when they are essential to an understanding of that passage. There are no rules for selecting the keywords. Searching for other occurrences of the keywords in Scripture in a concordance is necessary to understand the word's usage; this must be done in either Hebrew or Greek, not in English. A classic Hebraic approach is to find the usage of a word in the Scripture by finding other verses that contain the word. The usage of a word, in its original language, is discovered by searching the Scripture in the language of the word. Verses that contain the word are identified, and a pattern for the usage of the word discovered. Each verse is examined to see what the usage of the word is which, may reveal a model for the word's usage. For Hebrew words, the first usage of the word in the Scripture, primarily if used in the Torah, is essential. For the Greek words, the Christian Scriptures are used to determine the word usage in the Scripture. Sometimes finding the equivalent Greek word in the Septuagint then analyzing its usage in Hebrew can be very helpful.

The Rules of Hillel are used when applicable. Hillel was a Torah scholar who lived shortly before Yeshua's day. Hillel developed several rules for Torah students to interpret the Scriptures which refer to halachic Midrash. In several cases, these rules are helpful in the analysis of the Scripture.

The cultural implications from the period of the writing are done after the linguistic analysis is completed. The culture is crucial because it is not explicitly referenced in the biblical narratives, as indicated earlier.

From the linguistic analysis and the cultural understanding, it is possible to obtain a deeper meaning of the Scripture beyond the literal meaning of the plain text. That is what the listeners of Yeshua's time were doing. They put the linguistics and culture together without even having to contemplate it. They did it.

The analysis will lead to a set of findings explaining what the passage meant in Yeshua's day. Most of the time, the Hebraic analysis leads to the desire for more in-depth analysis to fully understand what Yeshua was talking about or what was happening to Him. Whatever the result, a new, more in-depth understanding of the Scripture is obtained.

The components of the Process of Discovery are:

Language

  Process of Discovery

    Linguistics Section

      Linguistic Structure

      Discussion

      Questioning the Passage

      Verse Comparison of citations or proof text

      Translation Inconsistencies

      Biblical Personalities

      Biblical Locations

      Phrase Study

      Scripture cross-references

      Linguistic Echoes

      Rules of Hillel

Culture Section

Discussion

Questioning the passage

Cultural Echoes

Culture and Linguistics Section

Discussion

Thoughts

Reflections

Only the application sections are included in this document.

Chapter One

Language

New American Standard 1995	Hebrew
1 Now in the first year of Cyrus king of Persia, in order to fulfill the word of the LORD by the mouth of Jeremiah, the LORD stirred up the spirit of Cyrus king of Persia, so that he sent a proclamation throughout all his kingdom, and also *put it* in writing, saying: 2 "Thus says Cyrus king of Persia, 'The LORD, the God of heaven, has given me all the kingdoms of the earth and He has appointed me to build Him a house in Jerusalem, which is in Judah. 3 'Whoever there is among you of all His people, may his God be with him! Let him go up to Jerusalem which is in Judah and rebuild the house of the LORD, the God of Israel; He is the God who is in Jerusalem. 4 'Every survivor, at whatever place he may live, let the men of that place support him with silver and gold, with goods and cattle, together with a freewill offering for the house of God which is in Jerusalem.'" 5 Then the heads of fathers' *households* of Judah and Benjamin and the priests and the Levites arose, even everyone whose spirit God had stirred to go up and rebuild the house of the LORD which is in Jerusalem. 6 All those about them encouraged them with articles of silver, with gold, with goods, with cattle and with valuables, aside from all that was given as a freewill offering.	וּבִשְׁנַת אַחַת לְכוֹרֶשׁ מֶלֶךְ פָּרַס לִכְלוֹת דְּבַר־יְהוָה מִפִּי יִרְמְיָה הֵעִיר יְהוָה אֶת־רוּחַ כֹּרֶשׁ מֶלֶךְ־פָּרַס וַיַּעֲבֶר־קוֹל בְּכָל־מַלְכוּתוֹ וְגַם־בְּמִכְתָּב לֵאמֹר׃ 2 כֹּה אָמַר כֹּרֶשׁ מֶלֶךְ פָּרַס כֹּל מַמְלְכוֹת הָאָרֶץ נָתַן לִי יְהוָה אֱלֹהֵי הַשָּׁמָיִם וְהוּא־פָקַד עָלַי לִבְנוֹת־לוֹ בַיִת בִּירוּשָׁלַ͏ִם אֲשֶׁר בִּיהוּדָה׃ 3 מִי־בָכֶם מִכָּל־עַמּוֹ יְהִי אֱלֹהָיו עִמּוֹ וְיַעַל לִירוּשָׁלַ͏ִם אֲשֶׁר בִּיהוּדָה וְיִבֶן אֶת־בֵּית יְהוָה אֱלֹהֵי יִשְׂרָאֵל הוּא הָאֱלֹהִים אֲשֶׁר בִּירוּשָׁלָ͏ִם׃ 4 וְכָל־הַנִּשְׁאָר מִכָּל־הַמְּקֹמוֹת אֲשֶׁר הוּא גָר־שָׁם יְנַשְּׂאוּהוּ אַנְשֵׁי מְקֹמוֹ בְּכֶסֶף וּבְזָהָב וּבִרְכוּשׁ וּבִבְהֵמָה עִם־הַנְּדָבָה לְבֵית הָאֱלֹהִים אֲשֶׁר בִּירוּשָׁלָ͏ִם׃ 5 וַיָּקוּמוּ רָאשֵׁי הָאָבוֹת לִיהוּדָה וּבִנְיָמִן וְהַכֹּהֲנִים וְהַלְוִיִּם לְכֹל הֵעִיר הָאֱלֹהִים אֶת־רוּחוֹ לַעֲלוֹת לִבְנוֹת אֶת־בֵּית יְהוָה אֲשֶׁר בִּירוּשָׁלָ͏ִם׃ 6 וְכָל־סְבִיבֹתֵיהֶם חִזְּקוּ בִידֵיהֶם בִּכְלֵי־כֶסֶף בַּזָּהָב בָּרְכוּשׁ וּבַבְּהֵמָה וּבַמִּגְדָּנוֹת לְבַד עַל־כָּל־הִתְנַדֵּב׃ ס

7 Also King Cyrus brought out the articles of the house of the LORD, which Nebuchadnezzar had carried away from Jerusalem and put in the house of his gods;

8 and Cyrus, king of Persia, had them brought out by the hand of Mithredath the treasurer, and he counted them out to Sheshbazzar, the prince of Judah.

9 Now this *was* their number: 30 gold dishes, 1,000 silver dishes, 29 duplicates;

10 30 gold bowls, 410 silver bowls of a second *kind and* 1,000 other articles.

11 All the articles of gold and silver *numbered* 5,400. Sheshbazzar brought them all up with the exiles who went up from Babylon to Jerusalem.

וְהַמֶּ֣לֶךְ כּ֗וֹרֶשׁ הוֹצִיא֙ אֶת־כְּלֵ֣י בֵית־7 יְהוָ֔ה אֲשֶׁ֥ר הוֹצִ֖יא נְבֽוּכַדְנֶצַּ֣ר מִירֽוּשָׁלִַ֑ם וַיִּתְּנֵ֖ם בְּבֵ֥ית אֱלֹהָֽיו׃ וַיּֽוֹצִיאֵ֗ם כּ֚וֹרֶשׁ מֶ֣לֶךְ פָּרַ֔ס עַל־יַ֖ד8 מִתְרְדָ֣ת הַגִּזְבָּ֑ר וַיִּסְפְּרֵם֙ לְשֵׁשְׁבַּצַּ֔ר הַנָּשִׂ֖יא לִיהוּדָֽה׃ וְאֵ֖לֶּה מִסְפָּרָ֑ם אֲגַרְטְלֵ֨י זָהָ֜ב שְׁלֹשִׁ֗ים9 אֲגַרְטְלֵי־כֶ֤סֶף אֶ֙לֶף֙ מַחֲלָפִ֔ים תִּשְׁעָ֥ה וְעֶשְׂרִֽים׃ ס כְּפוֹרֵ֤י זָהָב֙ שְׁלֹשִׁ֔ים כְּפוֹרֵ֥י כֶ֙סֶף֙10 מִשְׁנִ֔ים אַרְבַּ֥ע מֵא֖וֹת וַעֲשָׂרָ֑ה כֵּלִ֥ים אֲחֵרִ֖ים אָֽלֶף׃ ס כָּל־כֵּלִים֙ לַזָּהָ֣ב וְלַכֶּ֔סֶף חֲמֵ֥שֶׁת11 אֲלָפִ֖ים וְאַרְבַּ֣ע מֵא֑וֹת הַכֹּ֞ל הֶעֱלָ֣ה שֵׁשְׁבַּצַּ֗ר עִ֚ם הֵעָל֣וֹת הַגּוֹלָ֔ה מִבָּבֶ֖ל לִירֽוּשָׁלִָֽם׃ פ

Process of Discovery

Linguistics Section

Linguistic Structure

A [1] Now in the first year of Cyrus king of Persia, in order to fulfill the word of the LORD by the mouth of Jeremiah, the LORD stirred up the spirit of Cyrus king of Persia, so that he sent a proclamation throughout all his kingdom, and also *put it* in writing, saying: [2] "Thus says Cyrus king of Persia, 'The LORD, the God of heaven, has given me all the kingdoms of the earth and He has appointed me to build Him a house in Jerusalem, which is in Judah. [3] 'Whoever there is among you of all His people, may his God be with him! Let him go up to Jerusalem which is in Judah and rebuild the house of the LORD, the God of Israel; He is the God who is in Jerusalem. [4] 'Every survivor, at whatever place he may live, let the men of that place support him with silver and gold, with goods and cattle, together with a freewill offering for the house of God which is in Jerusalem.'"

> **B** [5] Then the heads of fathers' *households* of Judah and Benjamin and the priests and the Levites arose, even everyone whose spirit God had stirred to go up and rebuild the house of the LORD which is in Jerusalem. [6] All those about them encouraged them with articles of silver, with gold, with goods, with cattle and with valuables, aside from all that was given as a freewill offering.

A' [7] Also King Cyrus brought out the articles of the house of the LORD, which Nebuchadnezzar had carried away from Jerusalem and put in the house of his gods; [8] and Cyrus, king of Persia, had them brought out by the hand of Mithredath the treasurer, and he counted them out to Sheshbazzar, the prince of Judah. [9] Now this *was* their number: 30 gold dishes, 1,000 silver dishes, 29 duplicates; [10] 30 gold bowls, 410 silver bowls of a second *kind and* 1,000 other articles. [11] All the articles of gold and silver *numbered* 5,400. Sheshbazzar brought them all up with the exiles who went up from Babylon to Jerusalem.

Discussion

This chapter is a simple chiasm that was determined by the two decrees of King Cyrus.

Questioning the Passage

1. When was the first year of the reign of Cyrus, king of Persia? (v. 1)

   The first year of the reign of Cyrus was 539 BCE. The decree could have been issued in 539 BCE.[9]

2. What does it mean to fulfill the word of the LORD by the mouth of Jeremiah? (v. 1)

   The LORD spoke through the prophet Jeremiah telling the Hebrew people that they were to be in Exile from Jerusalem and Judea for seventy years. The seventy years started after the second Babylonian invasion when the Temple at Jerusalem was destroyed.

3. What does it mean that the LORD stirred Cyrus' spirit? (v. 1)

   The Sage Ralbag[i] said that he believed that the LORD spoke to Cyrus in a dream. The LORD told Cyrus that he was given all the kingdoms on the Earth. Cyrus' payment to the LORD for his empire was to rebuild the LORD's house in Jerusalem.[10]

4. Why did the LORD anoint a pagan King to rebuild Jerusalem and the Temple? (v. 2)

   In a way, the LORD did not have a choice. His people were in Exile in Babylon. Cyrus was the king of Persia at the time. The seventy years of Exile was over. Israel had no possible way to defeat the Persians. Therefore, the LORD used the Persian King to accomplish His promise to His people.

---

[9] H. G. M. Williamson, *Word Biblical Commentary* , vol. 16 (Waco, TX: Word Books, 1985).

[10] Nosson Scherman and Meir Zlotowitz, *The Writings = Kesuvim / The Writings: with a Commentary Anthologized from Rabbinic Writings = Ketuvim: ʻim Perush Rashi, Metsudat Dayid, Metsudat Tsiyon, ye-ʻod* (Brooklyn, NY: Mesorah Publications, 2016).

Cyrus allowed them to return to Jerusalem and rebuild the Temple. The seventy-year Exile was over.

5. Could Cyrus say the sacred name of the LORD? (v. 2)

Cyrus was acknowledging the God of Israel. It is not clear if he said the name of the LORD. Probably, he never heard the pronunciation of the LORD's name. A question of historical significance is that the High Priest was only allowed to say out loud the LORD's name on Yom Kippur at 3:00 PM in the Holy of Holies of Jerusalem. How did the name's pronunciation get passed to the next generation while the people were in Babylon? The name today is pronounced "Adonai."

6. Why did Cyrus tell his people to give offerings to the Hebrew people who went to Jerusalem? (v. 4)

The Sages believe that Cyrus told the Hebrew people and some of his people to go to Jerusalem. They were assisting the Hebrew people in the rebuilding of the Temple at Jerusalem. When the Persian people went to Jerusalem, they were told to offer silver and gold so that the Hebrew people could acquire the tools and materials they needed to rebuild the Temple.

7. Who were the heads of the households of Judah and Benjamin? (v. 5)

The people who returned to Jerusalem are listed in chapter two.

8. Why are the priests and Levites mentioned separately? (v. 5)

Not all Levites were priests, but all priests were Levites. There was a distinction made between which Levites were and were not priests. The priests were descendants of Zadok, who was a descendant of Aaron. When

Zadok became High Priest, he changed how his successor was selected. The tradition became that the bloodline of Aaron was the only clan that could be priests in Israel.

9. Is there a significance to the number of artifacts that Cyrus had from the first Temple? (v. 9 & 10)

There does not appear to be a connection to the number of each item mentioned. The large number says that the items represented a large number of valuables. Gold and silver was used as money. Cyrus gave back a large sum of money to the Hebrews.

Biblical Personalities

1. Cyrus the Great, "also called Cyrus II, (born 590–580 BCE, Media, or Persis [now in Iran]—died c. 529, Asia), conqueror who founded the Achaemenian empire, centred on Persia and comprising the Near East from the Aegean Sea eastward to the Indus River. He is also remembered in the Cyrus legend—first recorded by Xenophon, Greek soldier and author, in his *Cyropaedia*—as a tolerant and ideal monarch who was called the father of his people by the ancient Persians. In the Bible he is the liberator of the Jews who were captive in Babylonia."[11]

2. Mithredath – "The treasurer of Cyrus king of Persia, to whom the king gave the vessels of the temple."[12]

---

[11] "Cyrus the Great," Encyclopædia Britannica (Encyclopædia Britannica, inc.), accessed January 9, 2021, https://www.britannica.com/biography/Cyrus-the-great.
[12] Topical Bible: Mithredath, accessed January 22, 2021, https://biblehub.com/topical/m/mithredath.htm.

3. Nebuchadnezzar "(Nebuchadrezzar), son of Nabopolassar the Chaldean, was the Babylonian ruler who reigned over much of the civilized world in 604-562 BCE. Nebuchadnezzar is notorious for decimating the Jewish presence in the Land of Israel, exiling the vast majority of its denizens to Babylon, and destroying the first Holy Temple."[13]

4. Sheshbazzar – "In 538 B.C., Cyrus appointed Sheshbazzar to lead an expedition of the first group of Israelites to return to Jerusalem from Babylon. He also entrusted Sheshbazzar with the task of returning the gold and silver vessels taken from the temple by Nebuchadnezzar during the Babylonian exile: "Moreover, King Cyrus brought out the articles belonging to the temple of the LORD, which Nebuchadnezzar had carried away from Jerusalem and had placed in the temple of his god. Cyrus king of Persia had them brought by Mithredath the treasurer, who counted them out to Sheshbazzar the prince of Judah. . . . In all, there were 5,400 articles of gold and of silver. Sheshbazzar brought all these along with the exiles when they came up from Babylon to Jerusalem" (Ezra 1:7–11)."[14]

Biblical Locations

1. Jerusalem "is the capital of the modern nation of Israel and a major holy city for the three Western traditions of Judaism, Christianity, and Islam. It sits on spurs of bedrock between the Mediterranean Sea and the Dead Sea area. To the north and west, it tapers off to the Jezreel Valley and the hills of the Galilee, while to the south lies the Judean desert. The city is

---

[13] Avrohom Bergstein, "Nebuchadnezzar The Evil Babylonian King Who Destroyed Jerusalem," Chabad, accessed January 25, 2021, https://www.chabad.org/library/article_cdo/aid/4451665/jewish/Nebuchadnezzar.htm.
[14] GotQuestions.org, "Home," GotQuestions.org, August 13, 2018, https://www.gotquestions.org/Sheshbazzar-in-the-Bible.html.

surrounded by three steep ravines (to the east, south, and west). On the other side of the eastern ravine, across the Kidron valley, is the Mount of Olives.

Historically, Jerusalem was an urban center for approximately 5,000 years. Scholars debate the original meaning of the name (Sumerian "foundation" or Semitic "to found" or to "lay a cornerstone"). It could also derive from the name of the Canaanite god of dusk, Shalem, where the main consonants of s-l-m also denote the Hebrew (*salam* or *shalom*), which means "peace." Ironically, the city has known very little peace over the centuries.

Today, Jerusalem consists of the modern, western section, built up after the institution of the state of Israel in 1948 CE, and the medieval section, known as the Old City, which is surrounded by walls and gates built during the reign of Suleiman I (1494-1566 CE) when the province was part of the Ottoman Empire. The Old City is divided into four quarters: the Jewish Quarter; the Christian Quarter; the Muslim Quarter; and the Armenian Quarter."[15]

Phrase Study

1. יְהוָה אֱלֹהֵי הַשָּׁמַיִם means "Yaweh God of Heaven." Cyrus does not acknowledge that the LORD is also the God of Earth. Since Persia had its own set of god's, he probably believed that his god was Earth's god. However, he acknowledged Israel's God as the God who controlled Heaven, but not Earth. There is a contradiction because Cyrus

---

[15] Rebecca Denova, "Jerusalem," Ancient History Encyclopedia (Ancient History Encyclopedia, January 9, 2021), https://www.ancient.eu/jerusalem/.

acknowledged that the LORD of Heaven did give him the kingdoms of Earth. How could Cyrus acknowledge this gift from the LORD and then call Him the God of Heaven? Cyrus also obeyed the command of the LORD of Heaven. It is unclear from the text how to solve this apparent contradiction. Perhaps Cyrus believed that the God of Heaven was more powerful than his god of Earth. Therefore, he felt compelled to do as the LORD asked.

Thoughts

In Persia's ancient world, the God of Israel was seen as a God of extreme power. The Persians were not monotheistic. Cyrus did acknowledge the LORD of Heaven, who had a deep influence on his god of the Earth. Cyrus gave Israel its freedom and money to rebuild the great city of Jerusalem and the Temple of the LORD because he believed that the LORD gave him power over every kingdom on Earth. One could say that Cyrus paid for the blessings from the LORD. Cyrus had a healthy reign because he paid tribute to the LORD.

Chapter Two

Language

New American Standard 1995	Hebrew
[1] Now these are the people of the province who came up out of the captivity of the exiles whom Nebuchadnezzar the king of Babylon had carried away to Babylon, and returned to Jerusalem and Judah, each to his city. [2] These came with Zerubbabel, Jeshua, Nehemiah, Seraiah, Reelaiah, Mordecai, Bilshan, Mispar, Bigvai, Rehum *and* Baanah. The number of the men of the people of Israel: [3] the sons of Parosh, 2,172; [4] the sons of Shephatiah, 372; [5] the sons of Arah, 775; [6] the sons of Pahath-moab of the sons of Jeshua *and* Joab, 2,812; [7] the sons of Elam, 1,254; [8] the sons of Zattu, 945; [9] the sons of Zaccai, 760; [10] the sons of Bani, 642; [11] the sons of Bebai, 623; [12] the sons of Azgad, 1,222; [13] the sons of Adonikam, 666; [14] the sons of Bigvai, 2,056; [15] the sons of Adin, 454; [16] the sons of Ater of Hezekiah, 98; [17] the sons of Bezai, 323; [18] the sons of Jorah, 112; [19] the sons of Hashum, 223; [20] the sons of Gibbar, 95; [21] the men of Bethlehem, 123; [22] the men of Netophah, 56; [23] the men of Anathoth, 128; [24] the sons of Azmaveth, 42;	וְאֵ֣לֶּה ׀ בְּנֵ֣י הַמְּדִינָ֗ה הָעֹלִים֙ מִשְּׁבִ֣י הַגּוֹלָ֔ה אֲשֶׁ֣ר הֶגְלָ֗ה (נְבוּכַדְנֶצּוֹר) [נְבוּכַדְנֶצַּ֛ר] מֶֽלֶךְ־בָּבֶ֖ל לְבָבֶ֑ל וַיָּשׁ֗וּבוּ לִירוּשָׁלַ֤ם וִיהוּדָה֙ אִ֥ישׁ לְעִירֽוֹ׃ [2] אֲשֶׁר־בָּ֣אוּ עִם־זְרֻבָּבֶ֗ל יֵשׁ֡וּעַ נְ֠חֶמְיָה שְׂרָיָ֨ה רְֽעֵלָיָ֜ה מָרְדֳּכַ֥י בִּלְשָׁ֛ן מִסְפָּ֥ר בִּגְוַ֖י רְח֑וּם בַּעֲנָ֑ה מִסְפַּר֙ אַנְשֵׁ֔י עַ֖ם יִשְׂרָאֵֽל׃ ס [3] בְּנֵ֣י פַרְעֹ֔שׁ אַלְפַּ֕יִם מֵאָ֖ה שִׁבְעִ֥ים וּשְׁנָֽיִם׃ ס [4] בְּנֵ֣י שְׁפַטְיָ֔ה שְׁלֹ֥שׁ מֵא֖וֹת שִׁבְעִ֥ים וּשְׁנָֽיִם׃ ס [5] בְּנֵ֣י אָרַ֔ח שְׁבַ֥ע מֵא֖וֹת חֲמִשָּׁ֥ה וְשִׁבְעִֽים׃ ס [6] בְּנֵֽי־פַחַ֥ת מוֹאָ֛ב לִבְנֵ֥י יֵשׁ֖וּעַ יוֹאָ֑ב אַלְפַּ֕יִם שְׁמֹנֶ֥ה מֵא֖וֹת וּשְׁנֵ֥ים עָשָֽׂר׃ ס [7] בְּנֵ֣י עֵילָ֔ם אֶ֕לֶף מָאתַ֖יִם חֲמִשִּׁ֥ים וְאַרְבָּעָֽה׃ ס [8] בְּנֵ֣י זַתּ֔וּא תְּשַׁ֥ע מֵא֖וֹת וְאַרְבָּעִ֥ים וַחֲמִשָּֽׁה׃ ס [9] בְּנֵ֣י זַכָּ֔י שְׁבַ֥ע מֵא֖וֹת וְשִׁשִּֽׁים׃ ס [10] בְּנֵ֣י בָנִ֔י שֵׁ֥שׁ מֵא֖וֹת אַרְבָּעִ֥ים וּשְׁנָֽיִם׃ ס [11] בְּנֵ֣י בֵבָ֔י שֵׁ֥שׁ מֵא֖וֹת עֶשְׂרִ֥ים וּשְׁלֹשָֽׁה׃ ס [12] בְּנֵ֣י עַזְגָּ֔ד אֶ֕לֶף מָאתַ֖יִם עֶשְׂרִ֥ים וּשְׁנָֽיִם׃ ס [13] בְּנֵי֙ אֲדֹ֣נִיקָ֔ם שֵׁ֥שׁ מֵא֖וֹת שִׁשִּׁ֥ים וְשִׁשָּֽׁה׃ ס [14] בְּנֵ֣י בִגְוָ֔י אַלְפַּ֖יִם חֲמִשִּׁ֥ים וְשִׁשָּֽׁה׃ ס [15] בְּנֵ֣י עָדִ֔ין אַרְבַּ֥ע מֵא֖וֹת חֲמִשִּׁ֥ים וְאַרְבָּעָֽה׃ ס [16] בְּנֵֽי־אָטֵ֥ר לִֽיחִזְקִיָּ֖ה תִּשְׁעִ֥ים וּשְׁמֹנָֽה׃ ס [17] בְּנֵ֣י בֵצָ֔י שְׁלֹ֥שׁ מֵא֖וֹת עֶשְׂרִ֥ים וּשְׁלֹשָֽׁה׃ ס [18] בְּנֵ֣י יוֹרָ֔ה מֵאָ֖ה וּשְׁנֵ֥ים עָשָֽׂר׃ ס [19] בְּנֵ֣י חָשֻׁ֔ם מָאתַ֖יִם עֶשְׂרִ֥ים וּשְׁלֹשָֽׁה׃ ס [20] בְּנֵ֥י גִבָּ֖ר תִּשְׁעִ֥ים וַחֲמִשָּֽׁה׃ ס [21] בְּנֵ֣י בֵֽית־לָ֔חֶם מֵאָ֖ה עֶשְׂרִ֥ים וּשְׁלֹשָֽׁה׃ ס [22] אַנְשֵׁ֥י נְטֹפָ֖ה חֲמִשִּׁ֥ים וְשִׁשָּֽׁה׃ [23] אַנְשֵׁ֣י עֲנָת֔וֹת מֵאָ֖ה עֶשְׂרִ֥ים וּשְׁמֹנָֽה׃ ס

<table>
<tr>
<td valign="top">

25 the sons of Kiriath-arim, Chephirah and Beeroth, 743;

26 the sons of Ramah and Geba, 621;

27 the men of Michmas, 122;

28 the men of Bethel and Ai, 223;

29 the sons of Nebo, 52;

30 the sons of Magbish, 156;

31 the sons of the other Elam, 1,254;

32 the sons of Harim, 320;

33 the sons of Lod, Hadid and Ono, 725;

34 the men of Jericho, 345;

35 the sons of Senaah, 3,630.

36 The priests: the sons of Jedaiah of the house of Jeshua, 973;

37 the sons of Immer, 1,052;

38 the sons of Pashhur, 1,247;

39 the sons of Harim, 1,017.

40 The Levites: the sons of Jeshua and Kadmiel, of the sons of Hodaviah, 74.

41 The singers: the sons of Asaph, 128.

42 The sons of the gatekeepers: the sons of Shallum, the sons of Ater, the sons of Talmon, the sons of Akkub, the sons of Hatita, the sons of Shobai, in all 139.

43 The temple servants: the sons of Ziha, the sons of Hasupha, the sons of Tabbaoth,

44 the sons of Keros, the sons of Siaha, the sons of Padon,

45 the sons of Lebanah, the sons of Hagabah, the sons of Akkub,

46 the sons of Hagab, the sons of Shalmai, the sons of Hanan,

47 the sons of Giddel, the sons of Gahar, the sons of Reaiah,

48 the sons of Rezin, the sons of Nekoda, the sons of Gazzam,

49 the sons of Uzza, the sons of Paseah, the sons of Besai,

</td>
<td valign="top" dir="rtl">

24 בְּנֵי עַזְמָוֶת אַרְבָּעִים וּשְׁנָיִם: ס

25 בְּנֵי קִרְיַת עָרִים כְּפִירָה וּבְאֵרוֹת שְׁבַע מֵאוֹת וְאַרְבָּעִים וּשְׁלֹשָׁה: ס

26 בְּנֵי הָרָמָה וָגָבַע שֵׁשׁ מֵאוֹת עֶשְׂרִים וְאֶחָד: ס

27 אַנְשֵׁי מִכְמָס מֵאָה עֶשְׂרִים וּשְׁנָיִם: ס

28 אַנְשֵׁי בֵית־אֵל וְהָעָי מָאתַיִם עֶשְׂרִים וּשְׁלֹשָׁה: ס

29 בְּנֵי נְבוֹ חֲמִשִּׁים וּשְׁנָיִם: ס

30 בְּנֵי מַגְבִּישׁ מֵאָה חֲמִשִּׁים וְשִׁשָּׁה: ס

31 בְּנֵי עֵילָם אַחֵר אֶלֶף מָאתַיִם חֲמִשִּׁים וְאַרְבָּעָה: ס

32 בְּנֵי חָרִם שְׁלֹשׁ מֵאוֹת וְעֶשְׂרִים: ס

33 בְּנֵי־לֹד חָדִיד וְאוֹנוֹ שְׁבַע מֵאוֹת עֶשְׂרִים וַחֲמִשָּׁה:

34 בְּנֵי יְרֵחוֹ שְׁלֹשׁ מֵאוֹת אַרְבָּעִים וַחֲמִשָּׁה: ס

35 בְּנֵי סְנָאָה שְׁלֹשֶׁת אֲלָפִים וְשֵׁשׁ מֵאוֹת וּשְׁלֹשִׁים: ס

36 הַכֹּהֲנִים בְּנֵי יְדַעְיָה לְבֵית יֵשׁוּעַ תִּשַׁע מֵאוֹת שִׁבְעִים וּשְׁלֹשָׁה: ס

37 בְּנֵי אִמֵּר אֶלֶף חֲמִשִּׁים וּשְׁנָיִם: ס

38 בְּנֵי פַשְׁחוּר אֶלֶף מָאתַיִם אַרְבָּעִים וְשִׁבְעָה: ס

39 בְּנֵי חָרִם אֶלֶף וְשִׁבְעָה עָשָׂר: ס

40 הַלְוִיִּם בְּנֵי־יֵשׁוּעַ וְקַדְמִיאֵל לִבְנֵי הוֹדַוְיָה שִׁבְעִים וְאַרְבָּעָה: ס

41 הַמְשֹׁרְרִים בְּנֵי אָסָף מֵאָה עֶשְׂרִים וּשְׁמֹנָה:

פ

42 בְּנֵי הַשֹּׁעֲרִים בְּנֵי־שַׁלּוּם בְּנֵי־אָטֵר בְּנֵי־טַלְמוֹן בְּנֵי־עַקּוּב בְּנֵי חֲטִיטָא בְּנֵי שֹׁבָי הַכֹּל מֵאָה שְׁלֹשִׁים וְתִשְׁעָה: פ

43 הַנְּתִינִים בְּנֵי־צִיחָא בְנֵי־חֲשׂוּפָא בְּנֵי טַבָּעוֹת:

44 בְּנֵי־קֵרֹס בְּנֵי־סִיעֲהָא בְּנֵי פָדוֹן:

45 בְּנֵי־לְבָנָה בְנֵי־חֲגָבָה בְּנֵי עַקּוּב:

46 בְּנֵי־חָגָב בְּנֵי־(שַׁמְלַי) [שַׁלְמַי] בְּנֵי חָנָן:

</td>
</tr>
</table>

50 the sons of Asnah, the sons of Meunim, the sons of Nephisim,

51 the sons of Bakbuk, the sons of Hakupha, the sons of Harhur,

52 the sons of Bazluth, the sons of Mehida, the sons of Harsha,

53 the sons of Barkos, the sons of Sisera, the sons of Temah,

54 the sons of Neziah, the sons of Hatipha.

55 The sons of Solomon's servants: the sons of Sotai, the sons of Hassophereth, the sons of Peruda,

56 the sons of Jaalah, the sons of Darkon, the sons of Giddel,

57 the sons of Shephatiah, the sons of Hattil, the sons of Pochereth-hazzebaim, the sons of Ami.

58 All the temple servants and the sons of Solomon's servants were 392.

59 Now these are those who came up from Tel-melah, Tel-harsha, Cherub, Addan *and* Immer, but they were not able to give evidence of their fathers' households and their descendants, whether they were of Israel:

60 the sons of Delaiah, the sons of Tobiah, the sons of Nekoda, 652.

61 Of the sons of the priests: the sons of Habaiah, the sons of Hakkoz, the sons of Barzillai, who took a wife from the daughters of Barzillai the Gileadite, and he was called by their name.

62 These searched *among* their ancestral registration, but they could not be located; therefore they were considered unclean *and excluded* from the priesthood.

63 The governor said to them that they should not eat from the most holy things

מז בְּנֵי־גָזֵּל בְּנֵי־גַחַר בְּנֵי רְאָיָה׃

מח בְּנֵי־רְצִין בְּנֵי־נְקוֹדָא בְּנֵי גַזָּם׃

מט בְּנֵי־עֻזָּא בְנֵי־פָסֵחַ בְּנֵי בֵסָי׃

נ בְּנֵי־אַסְנָה בְנֵי־(מְעִינִים) [מְעוּנִים] בְּנֵי (נְפִיסִים) [נְפוּסִים]׃

נא בְּנֵי־בַקְבּוּק בְּנֵי־חֲקוּפָא בְּנֵי חַרְחוּר׃

נב בְּנֵי־בַצְלוּת בְּנֵי־מְחִידָא בְּנֵי חַרְשָׁא׃

נג בְּנֵי־בַרְקוֹס בְּנֵי־סִיסְרָא בְּנֵי־תָמַח׃

נד בְּנֵי נְצִיחַ בְּנֵי חֲטִיפָא׃

נה בְּנֵי עַבְדֵי שְׁלֹמֹה בְּנֵי־סֹטַי בְּנֵי־הַסֹּפֶרֶת בְּנֵי פְרוּדָא׃

נו בְּנֵי־יַעְלָה בְנֵי־דַרְקוֹן בְּנֵי גִדֵּל׃

נז בְּנֵי שְׁפַטְיָה בְנֵי־חַטִּיל בְּנֵי פֹּכֶרֶת הַצְּבָיִים בְּנֵי אָמִי׃

נח כָּל־הַנְּתִינִים וּבְנֵי עַבְדֵי שְׁלֹמֹה שְׁלֹשׁ מֵאוֹת תִּשְׁעִים וּשְׁנָיִם׃ ס

נט וְאֵלֶּה הָעֹלִים מִתֵּל מֶלַח תֵּל חַרְשָׁא כְּרוּב אַדָּן אִמֵּר וְלֹא יָכְלוּ לְהַגִּיד בֵּית־אֲבוֹתָם וְזַרְעָם אִם מִיִּשְׂרָאֵל הֵם׃

ס בְּנֵי־דְלָיָה בְנֵי־טוֹבִיָּה בְּנֵי נְקוֹדָא שֵׁשׁ מֵאוֹת חֲמִשִּׁים וּשְׁנָיִם׃ ס

סא וּמִבְּנֵי הַכֹּהֲנִים בְּנֵי חֳבַיָּה בְּנֵי הַקּוֹץ בְּנֵי בַרְזִלַּי אֲשֶׁר לָקַח מִבְּנוֹת בַּרְזִלַּי הַגִּלְעָדִי אִשָּׁה וַיִּקָּרֵא עַל־שְׁמָם׃

סב אֵלֶּה בִּקְשׁוּ כְתָבָם הַמִּתְיַחְשִׂים וְלֹא נִמְצָאוּ וַיְגֹאֲלוּ מִן הַכְּהֻנָּה׃

סג וַיֹּאמֶר הַתִּרְשָׁתָא לָהֶם אֲשֶׁר לֹא־יֹאכְלוּ מִקֹּדֶשׁ הַקֳּדָשִׁים עַד עֲמֹד כֹּהֵן לְאוּרִים וּלְתֻמִּים׃

סד כָּל־הַקָּהָל כְּאֶחָד אַרְבַּע רִבּוֹא אַלְפַּיִם שְׁלֹשׁ־מֵאוֹת שִׁשִּׁים׃

סה מִלְּבַד עַבְדֵיהֶם וְאַמְהֹתֵיהֶם אֵלֶּה שִׁבְעַת אֲלָפִים שְׁלֹשׁ מֵאוֹת שְׁלֹשִׁים וְשִׁבְעָה וְלָהֶם מְשֹׁרְרִים וּמְשֹׁרְרוֹת מָאתָיִם׃

סו סוּסֵיהֶם שְׁבַע מֵאוֹת שְׁלֹשִׁים וְשִׁשָּׁה פִּרְדֵיהֶם מָאתַיִם אַרְבָּעִים וַחֲמִשָּׁה׃

until a priest stood up with Urim and Thummim.

⁶⁴ The whole assembly numbered 42,360,

⁶⁵ besides their male and female servants who numbered 7,337; and they had 200 singing men and women.

⁶⁶ Their horses were 736; their mules, 245;

⁶⁷ their camels, 435; *their* donkeys, 6,720.

⁶⁸ Some of the heads of fathers' *households*, when they arrived at the house of the LORD which is in Jerusalem, offered willingly for the house of God to restore it on its foundation.

⁶⁹ According to their ability they gave to the treasury for the work 61,000 gold drachmas and 5,000 silver minas and 100 priestly garments.

⁷⁰ Now the priests and the Levites, some of the people, the singers, the gatekeepers and the temple servants lived in their cities, and all Israel in their cities.

גְּמַלֵּיהֶם אַרְבַּע מֵאוֹת שְׁלֹשִׁים וַחֲמִשָּׁה ‎⁶⁷
חֲמֹרִים שֵׁשֶׁת אֲלָפִים שְׁבַע מֵאוֹת וְעֶשְׂרִים׃ פ

וּמֵרָאשֵׁי הָאָבוֹת בְּבוֹאָם לְבֵית יְהוָה אֲשֶׁר ‎⁶⁸
בִּירוּשָׁלִָם הִתְנַדְּבוּ לְבֵית הָאֱלֹהִים לְהַעֲמִידוֹ
עַל־מְכוֹנוֹ׃

כְּכֹחָם נָתְנוּ לְאוֹצַר הַמְּלָאכָה זָהָב ‎⁶⁹
דַּרְכְּמוֹנִים שֵׁשׁ־רִבֹּאות וָאֶלֶף ס וְכֶסֶף מָנִים
חֲמֵשֶׁת אֲלָפִים וְכָתְנֹת כֹּהֲנִים מֵאָה׃ ס

וַיֵּשְׁבוּ הַכֹּהֲנִים וְהַלְוִיִּם וּמִן־הָעָם ‎⁷⁰
וְהַמְשֹׁרְרִים וְהַשּׁוֹעֲרִים וְהַנְּתִינִים בְּעָרֵיהֶם
וְכָל־יִשְׂרָאֵל בְּעָרֵיהֶם׃ ס

Process of Discovery

Linguistics Section

Linguistic Structure

A [1] Now these are the people of the province who came up out of the captivity of the exiles whom Nebuchadnezzar the king of Babylon had carried away to Babylon, and returned to Jerusalem and Judah, each to his city.

B [2] These came with Zerubbabel, Jeshua, Nehemiah, Seraiah, Reelaiah, Mordecai, Bilshan, Mispar, Bigvai, Rehum *and* Baanah. The number of the men of the people of Israel: [3] the sons of Parosh, 2,172; [4] the sons of Shephatiah, 372; [5] the sons of Arah, 775; [6] the sons of Pahath-moab of the sons of Jeshua *and* Joab, 2,812; [7] the sons of Elam, 1,254; [8] the sons of Zattu, 945; [9] the sons of Zaccai, 760; [10] the sons of Bani, 642; [11] the sons of Bebai, 623; [12] the sons of Azgad, 1,222; [13] the sons of Adonikam, 666; [14] the sons of Bigvai, 2,056; [15] the sons of Adin, 454; [16] the sons of Ater of Hezekiah, 98; [17] the sons of Bezai, 323; [18] the sons of Jorah, 112; [19] the sons of Hashum, 223; [20] the sons of Gibbar, 95; [21] the men of Bethlehem, 123; [22] the men of Netophah, 56; [23] the men of Anathoth, 128; [24] the sons of Azmaveth, 42; [25] the sons of Kiriath-arim, Chephirah and Beeroth, 743; [26] the sons of Ramah and Geba, 621; [27] the men of Michmas, 122; [28] the men of Bethel and Ai, 223; [29] the sons of Nebo, 52; [30] the sons of Magbish, 156; [31] the sons of the other Elam, 1,254; [32] the sons of Harim, 320; [33] the sons of Lod, Hadid and Ono, 725; [34] the men of Jericho, 345; [35] the sons of Senaah, 3,630. [36] The priests: the sons of Jedaiah of the house of Jeshua, 973; [37] the sons of Immer, 1,052; [38] the sons of Pashhur, 1,247; [39] the sons of Harim, 1,017. [40] The Levites: the sons of Jeshua and Kadmiel, of the sons of Hodaviah, 74. [41] The singers: the sons of Asaph, 128. [42] The sons of the gatekeepers: the sons of Shallum, the sons of Ater, the sons of Talmon, the sons of Akkub, the sons of Hatita, the sons of Shobai, in all 139. [43] The temple servants: the sons of Ziha, the sons of Hasupha, the sons of Tabbaoth, [44] the sons of Keros, the sons of Siaha, the sons of Padon, [45] the sons of Lebanah, the sons of Hagabah, the sons of Akkub, [46] the sons of Hagab, the sons of Shalmai, the sons of Hanan, [47] the sons of Giddel, the sons of Gahar, the sons of Reaiah, [48] the sons of Rezin, the sons of Nekoda, the sons of Gazzam, [49] the sons of Uzza, the sons of Paseah, the sons of Besai, [50] the sons of Asnah, the sons of Meunim, the sons of Nephisim, [51] the sons of Bakbuk, the sons of Hakupha, the sons of Harhur, [52] the sons of Bazluth, the sons of Mehida, the sons of Harsha, [53] the sons of Barkos, the sons of Sisera, the sons of Temah, [54] the sons of Neziah, the sons of Hatipha. [55] The sons of Solomon's servants: the sons of Sotai, the sons of Hassophereth, the sons of Peruda, [56] the sons of Jaalah, the sons of

Darkon, the sons of Giddel, [57] the sons of Shephatiah, the sons of Hattil, the sons of Pochereth-hazzebaim, the sons of Ami. [58] All the temple servants and the sons of Solomon's servants were 392. [59] Now these are those who came up from Tel-melah, Tel-harsha, Cherub, Addan *and* Immer, but they were not able to give evidence of their fathers' households and their descendants, whether they were of Israel: [60] the sons of Delaiah, the sons of Tobiah, the sons of Nekoda, 652. [61] Of the sons of the priests: the sons of Habaiah, the sons of Hakkoz, the sons of Barzillai, who took a wife from the daughters of Barzillai the Gileadite, and he was called by their name. [62] These searched *among* their ancestral registration, but they could not be located; therefore they were considered unclean *and excluded* from the priesthood. [63] The governor said to them that they should not eat from the most holy things until a priest stood up with Urim and Thummim. [64] The whole assembly numbered 42,360, [65] besides their male and female servants who numbered 7,337; and they had 200 singing men and women. [66] Their horses were 736; their mules, 245; [67] their camels, 435; *their* donkeys, 6,720.

A' [68] Some of the heads of fathers' *households*, when they arrived at the house of the LORD which is in Jerusalem, offered willingly for the house of God to restore it on its foundation. [69] According to their ability they gave to the treasury for the work 61,000 gold drachmas and 5,000 silver minas and 100 priestly garments. [70] Now the priests and the Levites, some of the people, the singers, the gatekeepers and the temple servants lived in their cities, and all Israel in their cities.

Discussion

This chapter identifies the people who returned to Jerusalem. The first Jews to return to Jerusalem were under the leadership of Zerubbabel and Jeshua in 538 CE. The second wave was with Ezra in 458 BCE. The third group came in 443 BCE.[16]

---

[16] Rocco A. Errico and George M. Lamsa, *Aramaic Light on Ezra through the Song of Solomon* (Smyma, GA: Noohra Foundation, 2010).

Thoughts

The book of Ezra has this list of the families that left Babylon and headed back to Jerusalem. The families had been in Babylon for seventy years and some longer because of the first Exile. These families abandoned whatever businesses or homes that they had built in their exiled home. Babylon and Susa became home to most people. The people returning would have been born in Exile. Thus, they never saw Jerusalem. They thought that returning was a sacred duty. The rebuilding of the LORD's house and His city was more important to them than their materialism in Babylon.

Chapter Three

Language

New American Standard 1995	Hebrew
[1] Now when the seventh month came, and the sons of Israel *were* in the cities, the people gathered together as one man to Jerusalem. [2] Then Jeshua the son of Jozadak and his brothers the priests, and Zerubbabel the son of Shealtiel and his brothers arose and built the altar of the God of Israel to offer burnt offerings on it, as it is written in the law of Moses, the man of God. [3] So they set up the altar on its foundation, for they were terrified because of the peoples of the lands; and they offered burnt offerings on it to the LORD, burnt offerings morning and evening. [4] They celebrated the Feast of Booths, as it is written, and *offered* the fixed number of burnt offerings daily, according to the ordinance, as each day required; [5] and afterward *there was* a continual burnt offering, also for the new moons and for all the fixed festivals of the LORD that were consecrated, and from everyone who offered a freewill offering to the LORD. [6] From the first day of the seventh month they began to offer burnt offerings to the LORD, but the foundation of the Temple of the LORD had not been laid. [7] Then they gave money to the masons and carpenters, and food, drink and oil to the Sidonians and to the Tyrians, to bring cedar wood from Lebanon to the sea at Joppa, according to the permission they had [1]from Cyrus king of Persia. [8] Now in the second year of their coming to the house of God at	וַיִּגַּע הַחֹדֶשׁ הַשְּׁבִיעִי וּבְנֵי יִשְׂרָאֵל בֶּעָרִים ס וַיֵּאָסְפוּ הָעָם כְּאִישׁ אֶחָד אֶל־יְרוּשָׁלָ͏ִם׃ ס 2 וַיָּקָם יֵשׁוּעַ בֶּן־יוֹצָדָק וְאֶחָיו הַכֹּהֲנִים וּזְרֻבָּבֶל בֶּן־שְׁאַלְתִּיאֵל וְאֶחָיו וַיִּבְנוּ אֶת־מִזְבַּח אֱלֹהֵי יִשְׂרָאֵל לְהַעֲלוֹת עָלָיו עֹלוֹת כַּכָּתוּב בְּתוֹרַת מֹשֶׁה אִישׁ־הָאֱלֹהִים׃ 3 וַיָּכִינוּ הַמִּזְבֵּחַ עַל־מְכוֹנֹתָיו כִּי בְּאֵימָה עֲלֵיהֶם מֵעַמֵּי הָאֲרָצוֹת וַיַּעַל [ו][וַיַּעֲלוּ] עָלָיו עֹלוֹת לַיהוָה עֹלוֹת לַבֹּקֶר וְלָעָרֶב׃ 4 וַיַּעֲשׂוּ אֶת־חַג הַסֻּכּוֹת כַּכָּתוּב וְעֹלַת יוֹם בְּיוֹם בְּמִסְפָּר כְּמִשְׁפַּט דְּבַר־יוֹם בְּיוֹמוֹ׃ 5 וְאַחֲרֵיכֵן עֹלַת תָּמִיד וְלֶחֳדָשִׁים וּלְכָל־מוֹעֲדֵי יְהוָה הַמְקֻדָּשִׁים וּלְכֹל מִתְנַדֵּב נְדָבָה לַיהוָה׃ 6 מִיּוֹם אֶחָד לַחֹדֶשׁ הַשְּׁבִיעִי הֵחֵלּוּ לְהַעֲלוֹת עֹלוֹת לַיהוָה וְהֵיכַל יְהוָה לֹא יֻסָּד׃ 7 וַיִּתְּנוּ־כֶסֶף לַחֹצְבִים וְלֶחָרָשִׁים וּמַאֲכָל וּמִשְׁתֶּה וָשֶׁמֶן לַצִּדֹנִים וְלַצֹּרִים לְהָבִיא עֲצֵי אֲרָזִים מִן־הַלְּבָנוֹן אֶל־יָם יָפוֹא כְּרִשְׁיוֹן כּוֹרֶשׁ מֶלֶךְ־פָּרַס עֲלֵיהֶם׃ פ 8 וּבַשָּׁנָה

Jerusalem in the second month, Zerubbabel the son of Shealtiel and Jeshua the son of Jozadak and the rest of their brothers the priests and the Levites, and all who came from the captivity to Jerusalem, began *the work* and appointed the Levites from twenty years and older to oversee the work of the house of the LORD. 9 Then Jeshua *with* his sons and brothers stood united *with* Kadmiel and his sons, the sons of Judah *and* the sons of Henadad *with* their sons and brothers the Levites, to oversee the workmen in the Temple of God. 10 Now when the builders had laid the foundation of the Temple of the LORD, the priests stood in their apparel with trumpets, and the Levites, the sons of Asaph, with cymbals, to praise the LORD according to the directions of King David of Israel. 11 They sang, praising and giving thanks to the LORD, *saying,* "For He is good, for His lovingkindness is upon Israel forever." And all the people shouted with a great shout when they praised the LORD because the foundation of the house of the LORD was laid. 12 Yet many of the priests and Levites and heads of fathers' *households,* the old men who had seen the first Temple, wept with a loud voice when the foundation of this house was laid before their eyes, while many shouted aloud for joy, 13 so that the people could not distinguish the sound of the shout of joy from the sound of the weeping of the people, for the people shouted with a loud shout, and the sound was heard far away.

הַשֵּׁנִית לְבוֹאָם אֶל־בֵּית הָאֱלֹהִים
לִירוּשָׁלַם בַּחֹדֶשׁ הַשֵּׁנִי הֵחֵלּוּ
זְרֻבָּבֶל בֶּן־שְׁאַלְתִּיאֵל וְיֵשׁוּעַ בֶּן־
יוֹצָדָק וּשְׁאָר אֲחֵיהֶם ׀ הַכֹּהֲנִים
וְהַלְוִיִּם וְכָל־הַבָּאִים מֵהַשְּׁבִי
יְרוּשָׁלַם וַיַּעֲמִידוּ אֶת־הַלְוִיִּם מִבֶּן
עֶשְׂרִים שָׁנָה וָמַעְלָה לְנַצֵּחַ עַל־
מְלֶאכֶת בֵּית־יְהוָה: פ 9 וַיַּעֲמֹד
יֵשׁוּעַ בָּנָיו וְאֶחָיו קַדְמִיאֵל וּבָנָיו
בְּנֵי־יְהוּדָה כְּאֶחָד לְנַצֵּחַ עַל־עֹשֵׂה
הַמְּלָאכָה בְּבֵית הָאֱלֹהִים ס בְּנֵי
חֵנָדָד בְּנֵיהֶם וַאֲחֵיהֶם הַלְוִיִּם: 10
וְיִסְּדוּ הַבֹּנִים אֶת־הֵיכַל יְהוָה
וַיַּעֲמִידוּ הַכֹּהֲנִים מְלֻבָּשִׁים
בַּחֲצֹצְרוֹת וְהַלְוִיִּם בְּנֵי־אָסָף
בַּמְצִלְתַּיִם לְהַלֵּל אֶת־יְהוָה עַל־
יְדֵי דָּוִיד מֶלֶךְ־יִשְׂרָאֵל: 11 וַיַּעֲנוּ
בְּהַלֵּל וּבְהוֹדֹת לַיהוָה כִּי טוֹב כִּי־
לְעוֹלָם חַסְדּוֹ עַל־יִשְׂרָאֵל וְכָל־
הָעָם הֵרִיעוּ תְרוּעָה גְדוֹלָה בְהַלֵּל
לַיהוָה עַל הוּסַד בֵּית־יְהוָה: ס 12
וְרַבִּים מֵהַכֹּהֲנִים וְהַלְוִיִּם וְרָאשֵׁי
הָאָבוֹת הַזְּקֵנִים אֲשֶׁר רָאוּ אֶת־
הַבַּיִת הָרִאשׁוֹן בְּיָסְדוֹ זֶה הַבַּיִת
בְּעֵינֵיהֶם בֹּכִים בְּקוֹל גָּדוֹל וְרַבִּים
בִּתְרוּעָה בְשִׂמְחָה לְהָרִים קוֹל: 13
וְאֵין הָעָם מַכִּירִים קוֹל תְּרוּעַת
הַשִּׂמְחָה לְקוֹל בְּכִי הָעָם כִּי הָעָם

	מְרִיעִים תְּרוּעָה גְדוֹלָה וְהַקּוֹל נִשְׁמַע עַד־לְמֵרָחוֹק: פ

Process of Discovery

Linguistics Section

Linguistic Structure

[The work of rebuilding] [1] Now when the seventh month came, and the sons of Israel *were* in the cities, the people gathered together as one man to Jerusalem. [2] Then Jeshua the son of Jozadak and his brothers the priests, and Zerubbabel the son of Shealtiel and his brothers arose and built the altar of the God of Israel to offer burnt offerings on it, as it is written in the law of Moses, the man of God. [3] So they set up the altar on its foundation, for they were terrified because of the peoples of the lands; and they offered burnt offerings on it to the LORD, burnt offerings morning and evening. [4] They celebrated the Feast of Booths, as it is written, and *offered* the fixed number of burnt offerings daily, according to the ordinance, as each day required; [5] and afterward *there was* a continual burnt offering, also for the new moons and for all the fixed festivals of the LORD that were consecrated, and from everyone who offered a freewill offering to the LORD. [6] From the first day of the seventh month they began to offer burnt offerings to the LORD, but the foundation of the Temple of the LORD had not been laid. [7] Then they gave money to the masons and carpenters, and food, drink and oil to the Sidonians and to the Tyrians, to bring cedar wood from Lebanon to the sea at Joppa, according to the permission they had [1]from Cyrus king of Persia. [8] Now in the second year of their coming to the house of God at Jerusalem in the second month, Zerubbabel the son of Shealtiel and Jeshua the son of Jozadak and the rest of their brothers the priests and the Levites, and all who came from the captivity to Jerusalem, began *the work* and appointed the Levites from twenty years and older to oversee the work of the house of the LORD. [9] Then Jeshua *with* his sons and brothers stood united *with* Kadmiel and his sons, the sons of Judah *and* the sons of Henadad *with* their sons and brothers the Levites, to oversee the workmen in the Temple of God. [10] Now when the builders had laid the foundation of the Temple of the LORD, the priests stood in their apparel with trumpets, and the Levites, the sons of Asaph, with cymbals, to praise the LORD according to the directions of King David of Israel. [11] They sang, praising and giving thanks to the LORD, *saying,* "For He is good, for His lovingkindness is upon Israel forever." And all the people shouted with a great shout when they praised the LORD because the foundation of the house of the LORD was laid. [12] Yet many of the priests and Levites and heads of fathers' *households,* the old men who had seen the first Temple, wept with a loud voice when the foundation of this house was laid before their eyes, while many shouted aloud for joy, [13] so that the people could not distinguish the sound of the shout of joy from the sound of the weeping of the people, for the people shouted with a loud shout, and the sound was heard far away.

Discussion

This chapter describes the work that was done for the rebuilding of the Temple in Jerusalem.

Questioning the Passage

1. When is the seventh month of the year? (v. 1)

   The seventh month is the month of Tishrei. Rosh HaShannah, Yom Kippur, and Succot are celebrated and observed in this month. It is considered the first month of the religious calendar. It was an appropriate month to commence the rebuilding of the spiritual center of ancient Judaism.

2. What does "the people were gathered together as one man" mean? (v. 1)

   The Israelites who returned from exile to rebuild the Temple were all together in Jerusalem. They worked together as a single-minded person. The rebuilding of the Temple was their mission.

3. Why were they terrified because of the peoples of the lands? (v. 3)

   The Sage Rashi[ii] said that they were terrified that the people who lived in Jerusalem would interfere with their labor and slander them by telling the Persian officials that nothing was happening. Therefore, an altar was quickly constructed according to the Torah.

4. What is the Feast of Booths (Succot)? (v. 4)

   "Sukkot is a weeklong Jewish holiday that comes five days after Yom Kippur. Sukkot celebrates the harvest and commemorates the miraculous protection G-d provided for the children of Israel when they left Egypt. We celebrate Sukkot by dwelling in a foliage-covered booth (known as a *sukkah*) and by taking the "Four Kinds" (*arba minim*), four special species of vegetation."[17]

5. What are the new moons? (v. 5)

   The new moon is the beginning of a new month.

6. What is the second month? (v. 8)

   The is the month of Iyar.[18]

Biblical Personalities

7. Jeshua – "in the Book of Ezra, Yeshua is the first High Priest of the Second Temple in Jerusalem. According to the Book of Ezra, Yeshua was instrumental in promoting the rebuilding of the Temple. After its construction, Yeshua served as its High Priest for at least two decades. Yeshua is also noted in the book because some of his relatives had sinned intermarriage with non-Jews. Yeshua may have lived to at least 90 years old. Yeshua is also mentioned in the Book of Zechariah."[19]

8. Zerubbabel – "Zerubbabel was an influential political and religious leader in Israel when Jewish exiles returned from captivity in Babylon. He's best

---

[17] Menachem Posner, "What Is Sukkot?," What is Sukkot?, accessed January 18, 2021, https://www.chabad.org/library/article_cdo/aid/4784/jewish/What-Is-Sukkot.htm.

[18] A. J. Rosenberg, *Daniel, Ezra, Nehemiah: a New English Translation = Sifrê Dānîyyēl, 'Ezrâ, Něhemyā* (New York: Judaica Pr., 1991).

[19] Study.com, accessed January 13, 2021, https://study.com/academy/answer/who-is-jeshua-in-the-book-of-ezra.html.

known for spearheading the rebuilding of God's Temple in Jerusalem in the 6th Century B.C."[20]

9. Kadamiel – "(before God), one of the Levites who with his family returned from Babylon with Zerubbabel. (Ezra 2:40; Nehemiah 7:43) He and his house are mentioned in history on three occasions - (Ezra 3:9; Nehemiah 9:4,5; 10:9) (B.C. 535-410.)"[21]

10. Henadad – "(grace of Hadad), the head of a family of the Levites who took a prominent part in the rebuilding of the temple. (Ezra 3:9)"[22]

11. Asaph – "A Levite; one of the leaders of David's choir (1 Chronicles 6:39). Psalms 50 and 73-83 inclusive are attributed to him. He is mentioned along with David as skilled in music, and a "seer" (2 Chronicles 29:30). The "sons of Asaph," mentioned in 1 Chronicles 25:1, 2 Chronicles 20:14, and Ezra 2:41, were his descendants, or more probably a class of poets or singers who recognized him as their master."[23]

Phrase Study

1. אִישׁ־הָאֱלֹהִים means "man of God." This is a person who follows the LORD's Will entirely and to the letter of the Torah.

---

[20] Mike Nappa, "Who Was Zerubbabel in the Bible?," Christianity.com (Salem Web Network, July 24, 2019), https://www.christianity.com/wiki/people/who-was-zerubbabel-in-the-bible.html.

[21] Topical Bible: Kadmiel, accessed January 22, 2021, https://biblehub.com/topical/k/kadmiel.htm.

[22] Topical Bible: Henadad, accessed January 22, 2021, https://biblehub.com/topical/h/henadad.htm.

[23] Topical Bible: Asaph, accessed January 22, 2021, https://biblehub.com/topical/a/asaph.htm.

Thoughts

The fantastic opportunity for the people who returned to Jerusalem came. They placed the foundational stones for the Second Temple. In the celebration, the people who saw the destruction of the First Temple were in tears. One should remember that even at a time of celebration, there are people who are weeping. Always consider their feelings.

Chapter Four

New American Standard 1995	Hebrew

¹ Now when the enemies of Judah and Benjamin heard that the people of the Exile were building a temple to the LORD God of Israel, **²** they approached Zerubbabel and the heads of fathers' *households,* and said to them, "Let us build with you, for we, like you, seek your God; and we have been sacrificing to Him since the days of Esarhaddon king of Assyria, who brought us up here." **³** But Zerubbabel and Jeshua and the rest of the heads of fathers' *households* of Israel said to them, "You have nothing in common with us in building a house to our God; but we ourselves will together build to the LORD God of Israel, as King Cyrus, the king of Persia has commanded us." **⁴** Then the people of the land discouraged the people of Judah, and frightened them from building, **⁵** and hired counselors against them to frustrate their counsel all the days of Cyrus king of Persia, even until the reign of Darius king of Persia. **⁶** Now in the reign of Ahasuerus, in the beginning of his reign, they wrote an accusation against the inhabitants of Judah and Jerusalem. **⁷** And in the days of Artaxerxes, Bishlam, Mithredath, Tabeel and the rest of his colleagues wrote to Artaxerxes king of Persia; and the text of the letter was written in Aramaic and translated *from* Aramaic. **⁸** Rehum the commander and Shimshai the scribe wrote a letter against Jerusalem to King Artaxerxes, as follows — **⁹** then *wrote*

וַיִּשְׁמְעוּ צָרֵי יְהוּדָה וּבִנְיָמִן כִּי־בְנֵי
הַגּוֹלָה בּוֹנִים הֵיכָל לַיהוָה אֱלֹהֵי
יִשְׂרָאֵל׃ ² וַיִּגְּשׁוּ אֶל־זְרֻבָּבֶל וְאֶל־
רָאשֵׁי הָאָבוֹת וַיֹּאמְרוּ לָהֶם נִבְנֶה
עִמָּכֶם כִּי כָכֶם נִדְרוֹשׁ לֵאלֹהֵיכֶם וְלֹא
[וְ][לוֹ] אֲנַחְנוּ זֹבְחִים מִימֵי אֵסַר חַדֹּן
מֶלֶךְ אַשּׁוּר הַמַּעֲלֶה אֹתָנוּ פֹּה׃ ³
וַיֹּאמֶר לָהֶם זְרֻבָּבֶל וְיֵשׁוּעַ וּשְׁאָר רָאשֵׁי
הָאָבוֹת לְיִשְׂרָאֵל לֹא־לָכֶם וָלָנוּ לִבְנוֹת
בַּיִת לֵאלֹהֵינוּ כִּי אֲנַחְנוּ יַחַד נִבְנֶה
לַיהוָה אֱלֹהֵי יִשְׂרָאֵל כַּאֲשֶׁר צִוָּנוּ
הַמֶּלֶךְ כּוֹרֶשׁ מֶלֶךְ־פָּרָס׃ ⁴ וַיְהִי עַם־
הָאָרֶץ מְרַפִּים יְדֵי עַם־יְהוּדָה
וּמְבַלֲהִים [וּ][מְבַהֲלִים] אוֹתָם לִבְנוֹת׃
⁵ וְסֹכְרִים עֲלֵיהֶם יוֹעֲצִים לְהָפֵר עֲצָתָם
כָּל־יְמֵי כּוֹרֶשׁ מֶלֶךְ פָּרַס וְעַד־מַלְכוּת
דָּרְיָוֶשׁ מֶלֶךְ־פָּרָס׃ ⁶ וּבְמַלְכוּת
אֲחַשְׁוֵרוֹשׁ בִּתְחִלַּת מַלְכוּתוֹ כָּתְבוּ
שִׂטְנָה עַל־יֹשְׁבֵי יְהוּדָה וִירוּשָׁלִָם׃ ס ⁷
וּבִימֵי אַרְתַּחְשַׁשְׂתָּא כָּתַב בִּשְׁלָם
מִתְרְדָת טָבְאֵל וּשְׁאָר כְּנָוֹתוֹ [כְּנָוֹתָיו]
עַל־אַרְתַּחְשַׁשְׂתָּא [אַרְתַּחְשַׁשְׂתְּ] מֶלֶךְ
פָּרָס וּכְתָב הַנִּשְׁתְּוָן כָּתוּב אֲרָמִית
וּמְתֻרְגָּם אֲרָמִית׃ פ ⁸ רְחוּם בְּעֵל־טְעֵם
וְשִׁמְשַׁי סָפְרָא כְּתַבוּ אִגְּרָה חֲדָה עַל־
יְרוּשְׁלֶם לְאַרְתַּחְשַׁשְׂתָּא מַלְכָּא כְּנֵמָא׃

Rehum the commander and Shimshai the scribe and the rest of their colleagues, the judges and the lesser governors, the officials, the secretaries, the men of Erech, the Babylonians, the men of Susa, that is, the Elamites, [10] and the rest of the nations which the great and honorable Osnappar deported and settled in the city of Samaria, and in the rest of the region beyond the River. Now [11] this is the copy of the letter which they sent to him: "To King Artaxerxes: Your servants, the men in the region beyond the River, and now [12] let it be known to the king that the Jews who came up from you have come to us at Jerusalem; they are rebuilding the rebellious and evil city and are finishing the walls and repairing the foundations. [13] "Now let it be known to the king, that if that city is rebuilt and the walls are finished, they will not pay tribute, custom or toll, and it will damage the revenue of the kings. [14] "Now because we [1]are in the service of the palace, and it is not fitting for us to see the king's dishonor, therefore we have sent and informed the king, [15] so that a search may be made in the record books of your fathers. And you will discover in the record books and learn that that city is a rebellious city and damaging to kings and provinces, and that they have incited revolt within it in past days; therefore that city was laid waste. [16] "We inform the king that if that city is rebuilt and the walls finished, as a result you will have no possession in *the province* beyond the River." [17] *Then* the king sent an answer to Rehum the commander, to Shimshai the scribe, and to the rest of their colleagues who live in

⁹ אֱדַיִן רְחוּם בְּעֵל־טְעֵם וְשִׁמְשַׁי סָפְרָא
וּשְׁאָר כְּנָוָתְהוֹן דִּינָיֵא וַאֲפַרְסַתְכָיֵא
טַרְפְּלָיֵא אֲפָרְסָיֵא אַרְכְּוָי [אַרְכְּוָי][א]
בָבְלָיֵא שׁוּשַׁנְכָיֵא דהוא [דֶּהָיֵא][א]
עֵלְמָיֵא : ¹⁰ וּשְׁאָר אֻמַּיָּא דִּי הַגְלִי
אָסְנַפַּר רַבָּא וְיַקִּירָא וְהוֹתֵב הִמּוֹ
בְּקִרְיָה דִּי שָׁמְרָיִן וּשְׁאָר עֲבַר־נַהֲרָה
וּכְעֶנֶת : ¹¹ דְּנָה פַּרְשֶׁגֶן אִגַּרְתָּא דִּי
שְׁלַחוּ עֲלוֹהִי עַל־אַרְתַּחְשַׁשְׂתְּא מַלְכָּא
עַבְדָיךְ אֱנָשׁ עֲבַר־נַהֲרָה וּכְעֶנֶת : פ ¹²
יְדִיעַ לֶהֱוֵא לְמַלְכָּא דִּי יְהוּדָיֵא דִּי
סְלִקוּ מִן־לְוָתָךְ עֲלֶינָא אֲתוֹ לִירוּשְׁלֶם
קִרְיְתָא מָרָדְתָּא וּבְאִישְׁתָּא
[וּ][בְאִישְׁתָּ][א] בָּנַיִן וְשׁוּרַיָ [וְ][שׁוּרַיָ][א]
אַשְׁכְלִּלוּ [שַׁכְלִילוּ] וְאֻשַּׁיָּא יַחִיטוּ : ¹³
כְּעַן יְדִיעַ לֶהֱוֵא לְמַלְכָּא דִּי הֵן קִרְיְתָא
דָךְ תִּתְבְּנֵא וְשׁוּרַיָּה יִשְׁתַּכְלְלוּן מִנְדָּה־
בְלוֹ וַהֲלָךְ לָא יִנְתְּנוּן וְאַפְּתֹם מַלְכִים
תְּהַנְזִק : ¹⁴ כְּעַן כָּל־קֳבֵל דִּי־מְלַח
הֵיכְלָא מְלַחְנָא וְעַרְוַת מַלְכָּא לָא
אֲרִיךְ לַנָא לְמֶחֱזֵא עַל־דְּנָה שְׁלַחְנָא
וְהוֹדַעְנָא לְמַלְכָּא : ¹⁵ דִּי יְבַקַּר בִּסְפַר־
דָּכְרָנַיָּא דִּי אֲבָהָתָךְ וּתְהַשְׁכַּח בִּסְפַר
דָּכְרָנַיָּא וְתִנְדַּע דִּי קִרְיְתָא דָךְ קִרְיָא
מָרָדָא וּמְהַנְזְקַת מַלְכִין וּמְדִנָן
וְאֶשְׁתַּדּוּר עָבְדִין בְּגַוַּהּ מִן־יוֹמָת עָלְמָא
עַל־דְּנָה קִרְיְתָא דָךְ הָחָרְבַת : ¹⁶
מְהוֹדְעִין אֲנַחְנָה לְמַלְכָּא דִּי הֵן קִרְיְתָא
דָךְ תִּתְבְּנֵא וְשׁוּרַיָּה יִשְׁתַּכְלְלוּן לָקֳבֵל
דְּנָה חֲלָק בַּעֲבַר נַהֲרָא לָא אִיתַי לָךְ :

Samaria and in the rest of *the provinces* beyond the River: "Peace. And now **18** the document which you sent to us has been translated and read before me. **19** "A decree has been issued by me, and a search has been made and it has been discovered that that city has risen up against the kings in past days, that rebellion and revolt have been perpetrated in it, **20** that mighty kings have ruled over Jerusalem, governing all *the provinces* beyond the River, and that tribute, custom and toll were paid to them. **21** "So, now issue a decree to make these men stop *work,* that this city may not be rebuilt until a decree is issued by me. **22** "Beware of being negligent in carrying out this *matter;* why should damage increase to the detriment of the kings?" **23** Then as soon as the copy of King Artaxerxes' document was read before Rehum and Shimshai the scribe and their colleagues, they went in haste to Jerusalem to the Jews and stopped them by force of arms. **24** Then work on the house of God in Jerusalem ceased, and it was stopped until the second year of the reign of Darius king of Persia.

פ **17** פִּתְגָמָא שְׁלַח מַלְכָּא עַל־רְחוּם
בְּעֵל־טְעֵם וְשִׁמְשַׁי סָפְרָא וּשְׁאָר
כְּנָוָתְהוֹן דִּי יָתְבִין בְּשָׁמְרָיִן וּשְׁאָר
עֲבַר־נַהֲרָה שְׁלָם וּכְעֶת : ס **18** נִשְׁתְּוָנָא
דִּי שְׁלַחְתּוּן עֲלֶינָא מְפָרַשׁ קֱרִי קָדָמָי :
19 וּמִנִּי שִׂים טְעֵם וּבַקַּרוּ וְהַשְׁכַּחוּ דִּי
קִרְיְתָא דָךְ מִן־יוֹמָת עָלְמָא עַל־מַלְכִין
מִתְנַשְּׂאָה וּמְרַד וְאֶשְׁתַּדּוּר מִתְעֲבֶד־
בַּהּ : **20** וּמַלְכִין תַּקִּיפִין הֲווֹ עַל־
יְרוּשְׁלֶם וְשַׁלִּיטִין בְּכֹל עֲבַר נַהֲרָה
וּמִדָּה בְלוֹ וַהֲלָךְ מִתְיְהֵב לְהוֹן : **21** כְּעַן
שִׂימוּ טְּעֵם לְבַטָּלָא גֻּבְרַיָּא אִלֵּךְ
וְקִרְיְתָא דָךְ לָא תִתְבְּנֵא עַד־מִנִּי
טַעְמָא יִתְּשָׂם : **22** וּזְהִירִין הֱווֹ שָׁלוּ
לְמֶעְבַּד עַל־דְּנָה לְמָה יִשְׂגֵּא חֲבָלָא
לְהַנְזָקַת מַלְכִין : ס **23** אֱדַיִן מִן־דִּי
פַּרְשֶׁגֶן נִשְׁתְּוָנָא דִּי אַרְתַּחְשַׁשְׁתְּא
[אַרְתַּחְשַׁשְׂתְּ] מַלְכָּא קֱרִי קֳדָם־רְחוּם
וְשִׁמְשַׁי סָפְרָא וּכְנָוָתְהוֹן אֲזַלוּ בִבְהִילוּ
לִירוּשְׁלֶם עַל־יְהוּדָיֵא וּבַטִּלוּ הִמּוֹ
בְּאֶדְרָע וְחָיִל : ס **24** בֵּאדַיִן בְּטֵלַת
עֲבִידַת בֵּית־אֱלָהָא דִּי בִּירוּשְׁלֶם וַהֲוָת
בָּטְלָא עַד שְׁנַת תַּרְתֵּין לְמַלְכוּת דָּרְיָוֶשׁ
מֶלֶךְ־פָּרָס : פ

Process of Discovery

Linguistics Section

Linguistic Structure

A **¹** Now when the enemies of Judah and Benjamin heard that the people of the Exile were building a temple to the LORD God of Israel, **²** they approached Zerubbabel and the heads of fathers' *households,* and said to them, "Let us build with you, for we, like you, seek your God; and we have been sacrificing to Him since the days of Esarhaddon king of Assyria, who brought us up here." **³** But Zerubbabel and Jeshua and the rest of the heads of fathers' *households* of Israel said to them, "You have nothing in common with us in building a house to our God; but we ourselves will together build to the LORD God of Israel, as King Cyrus, the king of Persia has commanded us." **⁴** Then the people of the land discouraged the people of Judah, and frightened them from building, **⁵** and hired counselors against them to frustrate their counsel all the days of Cyrus king of Persia, even until the reign of Darius king of Persia. **⁶** Now in the reign of Ahasuerus, in the beginning of his reign, they wrote an accusation against the inhabitants of Judah and Jerusalem.

B **⁷** And in the days of Artaxerxes, Bishlam, Mithredath, Tabeel and the rest of his colleagues wrote to Artaxerxes king of Persia; and the text of the letter was written in Aramaic and translated *from* Aramaic. **⁸** Rehum the commander and Shimshai the scribe wrote a letter against Jerusalem to King Artaxerxes, as follows — **⁹** then *wrote* Rehum the commander and Shimshai the scribe and the rest of their colleagues, the judges and the lesser governors, the officials, the secretaries, the men of Erech, the Babylonians, the men of Susa, that is, the Elamites, **¹⁰** and the rest of the nations which the great and honorable Osnappar deported and settled in the city of Samaria, and in the rest of the region beyond the River. Now **¹¹** this is the copy of the letter which they sent to him: "To King Artaxerxes: Your servants, the men in the region beyond the River, and now **¹²** let it be known to the king that the Jews who came up from you have come to us at Jerusalem; they are rebuilding the rebellious and evil city and are finishing the walls and repairing the foundations. **¹³** "Now let it be known to the king, that if that city is rebuilt and the walls are finished, they will not pay tribute, custom or toll, and it will damage the revenue of the kings. **¹⁴** "Now because we ¹are in the service of the palace, and it is not fitting for us to see the king's dishonor, therefore we have sent and informed the king, **¹⁵** so that a search may be made in the record books of your fathers. And you will discover in the record books and learn that that city is a rebellious city and damaging to kings and provinces, and that they have incited revolt within it in past days; therefore that city was laid waste. **¹⁶** "We inform the king that if that city is rebuilt and the walls finished, as a result you will have no possession in *the province* beyond the River."

B' **17** *Then* the king sent an answer to Rehum the commander, to Shimshai the scribe, and to the rest of their colleagues who live in Samaria and in the rest of *the provinces* beyond the River: "Peace. And now **18** the document which you sent to us has been translated and read before me. **19** "A decree has been issued by me, and a search has been made and it has been discovered that that city has risen up against the kings in past days, that rebellion and revolt have been perpetrated in it, **20** that mighty kings have ruled over Jerusalem, governing all *the provinces* beyond the River, and that tribute, custom and toll were paid to them. **21** "So, now issue a decree to make these men stop *work,* that this city may not be rebuilt until a decree is issued by me. **22** "Beware of being negligent in carrying out this *matter;* why should damage increase to the detriment of the kings?"

A' **23** Then as soon as the copy of King Artaxerxes' document was read before Rehum and Shimshai the scribe and their colleagues, they went in haste to Jerusalem to the Jews and stopped them by force of arms. **24** Then work on the house of God in Jerusalem ceased, and it was stopped until the second year of the reign of Darius king of Persia.

Discussion

This chapter consists of an A-B-A' chiasm. The sections are extensive. Israel was preparing to return to Jerusalem. They got some unexpected assistance.

Questioning the Passage

1. What is the region beyond the River? (v. 11)

    This is the land of the Trans-Euphrates and Cheeneth.

Biblical Personalities

1. Tribe of Judah – "The southern Kingdom of Judah thrived until 587/586 BC when it was overrun by the Babylonians, who carried off many of the inhabitants into Exile. When the Persians conquered Babylonia in 538 BC, Cyrus the Great allowed the Jews to return to their homeland. They soon set to work to replace the magnificent Temple of Jerusalem that the Babylonians had destroyed. The history of the Jews from that time forward is predominantly the history of the tribe of Judah."[24]

2. Tribe of Benjamin – "the tribe of Benjamin and the tribe of Judah are the only two tribes which maintain a steady presence throughout all of the Bible, including the New Testament. Its central role in Israel's rich past is reflected in the geography and location of its centralized allotment detailed in the annals of the Old Testament."[25]

3. Esarhaddon - "(reigned 681-669 BCE) was the third king of the Sargonid Dynasty of the Neo-Assyrian Empire. He was the youngest son of King Sennacherib (reigned 705-681 BCE), and his mother was not the queen but a concubine named Zakutu (also known as Naqia-Zakutu, c.701-668 BCE). Esarhaddon is mentioned in the Bible in II Kings 19:37, Isaiah 37:38, and Ezra 4:2. He is best known for rebuilding Babylon (which his father had destroyed) and for his military campaigns in Egypt. An avid follower of

---

[24] "Judah," Encyclopædia Britannica (Encyclopædia Britannica, inc.), accessed January 13, 2021, https://www.britannica.com/topic/Judah-Hebrew-tribe.
[25] "The Tribe of Benjamin," israel, accessed January 13, 2021, https://www.israel-a-history-of.com/tribe-of-benjamin.html.

astrology, he consulted oracles on a regular basis throughout his reign, far more than any other Assyrian king. He claimed the gods had ordained him to restore Babylon and cleverly omitted from his inscriptions anything that would implicate Sennacherib in the city's fall. In his other diplomatic letters he seems equally careful and maintained, then enlarged, the empire his father had left to him. He died on campaign in Egypt and left the throne to his son, Ashurbanipal."[26]

4. Ahasuerus "the Persian king of the Book of Esther, being identified by the rabbis with the one mentioned in Dan. ix. 1 as father of Darius, king of Media, and with the one mentioned in Ezra, iv. 6, is counted as one of the three kings of Biblical history who ruled over the entire globe, the other two being Ahab and Nebuchadnezzar (Meg. 11*a*; Targ. Sheni on Esth. i. 2 has four, counting also Solomon among them; see Meg. 11*b*). He was wicked from the beginning to the end of his reign."[27]

5. Artaxerxes I "(died 425 BC, Susa, Elam [now in Iran]), Achaemenid king of Persia (reigned 465–425 BC)."[28]

6. Bishlam – "The name Bishlam occurs only once in the Bible. Bishlam is one of three named of a larger group of men who worked for king Artaxerxes of Persia south of the river Euphrates, and who wrote a letter to their king to persuade him to order the Jews to stop repairing the city of Jerusalem (Ezra

---

[26] Joshua J. Mark, "Esarhaddon," Ancient History Encyclopedia (Ancient History Encyclopedia, January 11, 2021), https://www.ancient.eu/Esarhaddon/.

[27] "JewishEncyclopedia.com," AHASUERUS - JewishEncyclopedia.com, accessed January 22, 2021, http://www.jewishencyclopedia.com/articles/967-ahasuerus.

[28] "Artaxerxes I," Encyclopædia Britannica (Encyclopædia Britannica, inc.), accessed January 22, 2021, https://www.britannica.com/biography/Artaxerxes-I.

4:7). It worked and Artaxerxes ordered the work to stop, which it did until the second year of king Darius (Ezra 4:24)."[29]

7. Tabeel – "a Persian governor of Samaria, who joined others in the attempt to prevent the rebuilding of Jerusalem."[30]

8. Rehum – "The "chancellor" of Artaxerxes, who sought to stir him up against the Jews (Ezra 4:8-24) and prevent the rebuilding of the walls and the temple of Jerusalem."[31]

9. Shimshai – "the shining one, or sunny, the secretary of Rehum the chancellor, who took part in opposing the rebuilding of the temple after the Captivity."[32]

10. Erech - "Erech, Sumerian Uruk, Greek Orchoë, modern Tall al-Warkāʾ, ancient Mesopotamian city located northwest of Ur (Tall Al-Muqayyar) in southeastern Iraq."[33]

11. Osnappar – "OSNAPPAR, ŏs năp' ər (אָסְנַפַּר:). The name is found only in Ezra 4:10, in a letter written in Aram., sent by Rehum the commander and Shimshai the scribe, and the rest of their associates, to Artaxerxes, king of Persia, to urge him to stop the building of the walls of Jerusalem by the Jews.

---

[29] Abarim Publications, "The Amazing Name Bishlam: Meaning and Etymology," Abarim Publications (Abarim Publications), accessed January 22, 2021, https://www.abarim-publications.com/Meaning/Bishlam.html.
[30] "Tabeel Definition and Meaning - Bible Dictionary," biblestudytools.com, accessed January 22, 2021, https://www.biblestudytools.com/dictionary/tabeel/.
[31] "Rehum Definition and Meaning - Bible Dictionary," biblestudytools.com, accessed January 22, 2021, https://www.biblestudytools.com/dictionary/rehum/.
[32] "Shimshai Definition and Meaning - Bible Dictionary," biblestudytools.com, accessed January 22, 2021, https://www.biblestudytools.com/dictionary/shimshai/.
[33] "Erech," Encyclopædia Britannica (Encyclopædia Britannica, inc.), accessed January 22, 2021, https://www.britannica.com/place/Erech.

Osnappar is generally identified with Ashurbanipal (Akkad. *Assur-bãn-apal* = "Ashur has made a son") who succeeded his father Esarhaddon as king of Assyria in 669 B.C. He captured Thebes in Egypt in 663 B.C., and made punitive raids against the Syrians, Phoenicians, and Arabs. In 641 B.C. Ashurbanipal sacked Susa, capital of Elam, and therefore is thought to be Osnappar, who, the Samaritans claimed, had brought natives of Elam and Susa to their area (Ezra 4:9, 10)."[34]

Biblical Locations

1. Babylonia " (/ˌbæbɪˈloʊniə/) was an ancient Akkadian-speaking state and cultural area based in central-southern Mesopotamia (present-day Iraq and Syria). A small Amorite-ruled state emerged in 1894 BCE, which contained the minor administrative town of Babylon.[1] It was merely a small provincial town during the Akkadian Empire (2335–2154 BCE) but greatly expanded during the reign of Hammurabi in the first half of the 18th century BCE and became a major capital city. During the reign of Hammurabi and afterwards, Babylonia was called "the country of Akkad" (*Māt Akkadī* in Akkadian), a deliberate archaism in reference to the previous glory of the Akkadian Empire."[35]

2. Susa "also called Shushan, Greek Susiane, modern Shush, capital of Elam (Susiana) and administrative capital of the Achaemenian

---

[34] Osnappar - Encyclopedia of The Bible - Bible Gateway, accessed January 22, 2021, https://www.biblegateway.com/resources/encyclopedia-of-the-bible/Osnappar.
[35] "Babylonia," Wikipedia (Wikimedia Foundation, January 22, 2021), https://en.wikipedia.org/wiki/Babylonia.

king Darius I and his successors from 522 BCE. It was located at the foot of the Zagros Mountains near the bank of the Karkheh Kūr (Choaspes) River in the Khuzistan region of Iran."[36]

3. Elam (ites) "Elam included more than Khuzestan; it was a combination of the lowlands and the immediate highland areas to the north and east. Elamite strength was based on an ability to hold these various areas together under a coordinated government that permitted the maximum interchange of the natural resources unique to each region. Traditionally this was done through a federated governmental structure."[37]

4. Samaria – "Sandwiched between Galilee to the north and Judea to the south, the region of Samaria figured prominently in the history of Israel, but over the centuries it fell prey to foreign influences, a factor which drew scorn from neighboring Jews."[38]

5. Trans-Euphrates – "a river in SW Asia, flowing from E Turkey through Syria and Iraq, joining the Tigris to form the Shatt-al-Arab near the Persian Gulf. 1700 miles (2735 km) long."[39]

6. Cheeneth – the territory south of Trans-Euphrates.

---

[36] "Susa," Encyclopædia Britannica (Encyclopædia Britannica, inc.), accessed January 22, 2021, https://www.britannica.com/place/Susa.
[37] History of Iran: Elamite Empire, accessed January 22, 2021, http://www.iranchamber.com/history/elamite/elamite.php.
[38] Jack Zavada, "Ancient Samaria: Find Out How Jesus Approached Racism in His Day," Learn Religions, accessed January 22, 2021, https://www.learnreligions.com/history-of-samaria-4062174.
[39] "Trans-Euphrates," WordPanda, accessed January 22, 2021, https://wordpanda.net/definition/trans-euphrates.

Phrase Study

1. וְסֹכְרִים עֲלֵיהֶם יוֹעֲצִים - means "and hired counselors." Counselors were not hired. The "counselors" were people who could hinder or stop the work. Errico (Aramaic scholar) argues that in the Aramaic version, the word *malkaneh* has been confused with *mawkaneh*. *Mawkaneh* means hinderers. The word counselors does not fit into the narrative.[40]

Thoughts

The proponents of the rebuilding of the Temple at Jerusalem did everything they could to stop the work. It is believed that those who were against the work were relatives of Nebuchadnezzar, who destroyed the first Temple. If they allowed the second Temple to be built, then they were traitors to him.

---

[40] Rocco A. Errico and George M. Lamsa, *Aramaic Light on Ezra through the Song of Solomon* (Smyma, GA: Noohra Foundation, 2010).

Chapter Five

New American Standard 1995	Hebrew
¹ When the prophets, Haggai the prophet and Zechariah the son of Iddo, prophesied to the Jews who were in Judah and Jerusalem in the name of the God of Israel, who was over them, ² then Zerubbabel the son of Shealtiel and Jeshua the son of Jozadak arose and began to rebuild the house of God which is in Jerusalem; and the prophets of God were with them supporting them. ³ At that time Tattenai, the governor of *the province* beyond the River, and Shethar-bozenai and their colleagues came to them and spoke to them thus, "Who issued you a decree to rebuild this temple and to finish this structure?" ⁴ Then we told them accordingly what the names of the men were who were reconstructing this building. ⁵ But the eye of their God was on the elders of the Jews, and they did not stop them until a report could come to Darius, and then a written reply be returned concerning it. ⁶ *This is* the copy of the letter which Tattenai, the governor of *the province* beyond the River, and Shethar-bozenai and his colleagues the officials, who were beyond the River, sent to Darius the king. ⁷ They sent a report to him in which it was written thus: "To Darius the king, all peace. ⁸ "Let it be known to the king that we have gone to the province of Judah, to the house of the great God, which is being built with huge stones, and ¹beams are being laid in the walls; and this work is going on with great	וְהִתְנַבִּי חַגַּי נְבִיאָה [נְבִי]א] וּזְכַרְיָה בַר־עִדּוֹא נְבִיאַיָּא [נְבִי]א] עַל־יְהוּדָיֵא דִּי בִיהוּד וּבִירוּשְׁלֶם בְּשֻׁם אֱלָהּ יִשְׂרָאֵל עֲלֵיהוֹן׃ ס ² בֵּאדַיִן קָמוּ זְרֻבָּבֶל בַר־שְׁאַלְתִּיאֵל וְיֵשׁוּעַ בַּר־יוֹצָדָק וְשָׁרִיו לְמִבְנֵא בֵּית אֱלָהָא דִּי בִירוּשְׁלֶם וְעִמְּהוֹן נְבִיאַיָּא [נְבִי]א] דִי־אֱלָהָא מְסָעֲדִין לְהוֹן׃ פ ³ בֵּהּ זִמְנָא אֲתָא עֲלֵיהוֹן תַּתְּנַי פַּחַת עֲבַר־נַהֲרָה וּשְׁתַר בּוֹזְנַי וּכְנָוָתְהוֹן וְכֵן אָמְרִין לְהֹם מַן־שָׂם לְכֹם טְעֵם בַּיְתָא דְנָה לִבְּנֵא וְאֻשַּׁרְנָא דְנָה לְשַׁכְלָלָה׃ ס ⁴ אֱדַיִן כְּנֵמָא אֲמַרְנָא לְהֹם מַן־אִנּוּן שְׁמָהָת גֻּבְרַיָּא דִּי־דְנָה בִנְיָנָא בָּנַיִן׃ ⁵ וְעֵין אֱלָהֲהֹם הֲוָת עַל־שָׂבֵי יְהוּדָיֵא וְלָא־בַטִּלוּ הִמּוֹ עַד־ טַעְמָא לְדָרְיָוֶשׁ יְהָךְ וֶאֱדַיִן יְתִיבוּן נִשְׁתְּוָנָא עַל־דְּנָה׃ פ ⁶ פַּרְשֶׁגֶן אִגַּרְתָּא דִּי־שְׁלַח תַּתְּנַי ׀ פַּחַת עֲבַר־נַהֲרָה וּשְׁתַר בּוֹזְנַי וּכְנָוָתֵהּ אֲפַרְסְכָיֵא דִּי בַּעֲבַר נַהֲרָה עַל־ דָּרְיָוֶשׁ מַלְכָּא׃ ⁷ פִּתְגָמָא שְׁלַחוּ

care and is succeeding in their hands. 9 "Then we asked those elders and said to them thus, 'Who issued you a decree to rebuild this temple and to finish this structure?' 10 "We also asked them their names so as to inform you, and that we might write down the names of the men who were at their head. 11 "Thus they answered us, saying, 'We are the servants of the God of heaven and earth and are rebuilding the temple that was built many years ago, which a great king of Israel built and finished. 12 'But because our fathers had provoked the God of heaven to wrath, He gave them into the hand of Nebuchadnezzar king of Babylon, the Chaldean, *who* destroyed this temple and deported the people to Babylon. 13 'However, in the first year of Cyrus king of Babylon, King Cyrus issued a decree to rebuild this house of God. 14 'Also the gold and silver utensils of the house of God which Nebuchadnezzar had taken from the temple in Jerusalem, and brought them to the temple of Babylon, these King Cyrus took from the temple of Babylon and they were given to one whose name was Sheshbazzar, whom he had appointed governor. 15 'He said to him, "Take these utensils, go *and* deposit them in the temple in Jerusalem and let the house of God be rebuilt in its place." 16 'Then that Sheshbazzar came *and* laid the foundations of the house of God in Jerusalem; and from then until now it has been under construction and it is not *yet* completed.' 17 "Now if it pleases the king, let a search be conducted in the king's treasure house, which is there in Babylon, if it be that a decree was issued by King

אֱלָהִי וְכִדְנָה כְּתִיב בְּגַוֵּהּ לְדָרְיָ֫וֶשׁ
מַלְכָּא שְׁלָמָא כֹֽלָּא ׃ ס 8 יְדִ֫יעַ |
לֶהֱוֵא לְמַלְכָּא דִּי־אֲזַ֫לְנָא לִיהוּד
מְדִינְתָּא לְבֵית אֱלָהָא רַבָּא וְהוּא
מִתְבְּנֵא אֶבֶן גְּלָל וְאָע מִתְּשָׂם
בְּכֻתְלַיָּא וַעֲבִידְתָּא דָךְ אָסְפַּרְנָא
מִתְעַבְדָא וּמַצְלַח בְּיֶדְהֹם ׃ ס 9
אֱדַיִן שְׁאֵלְנָא לְשָׂבַיָּא אִלֵּךְ כְּנֵמָא
אֲמַרְנָא לְהֹם מַן־שָׂם לְכֹם טְעֵם
בַּיְתָא דְנָה לְמִבְנְיָה וְאֻשַּׁרְנָא דְנָה
לְשַׁכְלָלָה ׃ 10 וְאַף שְׁמָהָתְהֹם
שְׁאֵלְנָא לְהֹם לְהוֹדָעוּתָךְ דִּי נִכְתֻּב
שֻׁם־גֻּבְרַיָּא דִּי בְרָאשֵׁיהֹם ׃ ס 11
וּכְנֵמָא פִתְגָמָא הֲתִיבוּנָא לְמֵמַר
אֲנַחְנָא הִמּוֹ עַבְדוֹהִי דִּי־אֱלָהּ
שְׁמַיָּא וְאַרְעָא וּבָנַיִן בַּיְתָא דִּי־הֲוָא
בְנֵה מִקַּדְמַת דְּנָה שְׁנִין שַׂגִּיאָן
וּמֶלֶךְ לְיִשְׂרָאֵל רַב בְּנָהִי
וְשַׁכְלְלֵהּ ׃ 12 לָהֵן מִן־דִּי הַרְגִּזוּ
אֲבָהֳתַנָא לֶאֱלָהּ שְׁמַיָּא יְהַב הִמּוֹ
בְּיַד נְבוּכַדְנֶצַּר מֶלֶךְ־בָּבֶל כַּסְדָּיָא
[כַּסְדָּאָה] וּבַיְתָה דְנָה סַתְרֵהּ
וְעַמָּה הַגְלִי לְבָבֶל ׃ ס 13 בְּרַם
בִּשְׁנַת חֲדָה לְכוֹרֶשׁ מַלְכָּא דִּי בָבֶל
כּוֹרֶשׁ מַלְכָּא שָׂם טְעֵם בֵּית אֱלָהָא
דְנָה לִבְּנֵא ׃ 14 וְאַף מָאנַיָּא דִּי
בֵית־אֱלָהָא דִּי דַהֲבָה וְכַסְפָּא דִּי
נְבוּכַדְנֶצַּר הַנְפֵּק מִן־הֵיכְלָא דִּי

Cyrus to rebuild this house of God at Jerusalem; and let the king send to us his decision concerning this *matter*."

בִּירוּשְׁלֶם וְהֵיבֵל הִמּוֹ לְהֵיכְלָא דִּי
בְבָבֶל הַנְפֵּק הִמּוֹ כּוֹרֶשׁ מַלְכָּא מִן־
הֵיכְלָא דִּי בָבֶל וִיהִיבוּ לְשֵׁשְׁבַּצַּר
שְׁמֵהּ דִּי פֶחָה שָׂמֵהּ: 15 וַאֲמַר־לֵהּ
אֵלֶּה [אֵל] מָאנַיָּא שֵׂא אֵזֶל־אֲחֵת
הִמּוֹ בְּהֵיכְלָא דִּי בִירוּשְׁלֶם וּבֵית
אֱלָהָא יִתְבְּנֵא עַל־אַתְרֵהּ: ס 16
אֱדַיִן שֵׁשְׁבַּצַּר דֵּךְ אֲתָא יְהַב אֻשַּׁיָּא
דִּי־בֵית אֱלָהָא דִּי בִירוּשְׁלֶם וּמִן־
אֱדַיִן וְעַד־כְּעַן מִתְבְּנֵא וְלָא שְׁלִם:
17 וּכְעַן הֵן עַל־מַלְכָּא טָב יִתְבַּקַּר
בְּבֵית גִּנְזַיָּא דִּי־מַלְכָּא תַמָּה דִּי
בְּבָבֶל הֵן אִיתַי דִּי־מִן־כּוֹרֶשׁ
מַלְכָּא שִׂים טְעֵם לְמִבְנֵא בֵית־
אֱלָהָא דֵךְ בִּירוּשְׁלֶם וּרְעוּת מַלְכָּא
עַל־דְּנָה יִשְׁלַח עֲלֶינָא: ס

Process of Discovery

Linguistics Section

Linguistic Structure

[Situation] [1] When the prophets, Haggai the prophet and Zechariah the son of Iddo, prophesied to the Jews who were in Judah and Jerusalem in the name of the God of Israel, who was over them, [2] then Zerubbabel the son of Shealtiel and Jeshua the son of Jozadak arose and began to rebuild the house of God which is in Jerusalem; and the prophets of God were with them supporting them. [3] At that time Tattenai, the governor of *the province* beyond the River, and Shethar-bozenai and their colleagues came to them and spoke to them thus, "Who issued you a decree to rebuild this temple and to finish this structure?" [4] Then we told them accordingly what the names of the men were who were reconstructing this building. [5] But the eye of their God was on the elders of the Jews, and they did not stop them until a report could come to Darius, and then a written reply be returned concerning it.

[Letter to Darius from Tattenai] [6] *This is* the copy of the letter which Tattenai, the governor of *the province* beyond the River, and Shethar-bozenai and his colleagues the officials, who were beyond the River, sent to Darius the king. [7] They sent a report to him in which it was written thus: "To Darius the king, all peace. [8] "Let it be known to the king that we have gone to the province of Judah, to the house of the great God, which is being built with huge stones, and ¹beams are being laid in the walls; and this work is going on with great care and is succeeding in their hands. [9] "Then we asked those elders and said to them thus, 'Who issued you a decree to rebuild this temple and to finish this structure?' [10] "We also asked them their names so as to inform you, and that we might write down the names of the men who were at their head. [11] "Thus they answered us, saying, 'We are the servants of the God of heaven and earth and are rebuilding the temple that was built many years ago, which a great king of Israel built and finished. [12] 'But because our fathers had provoked the God of heaven to wrath, He gave them into the hand of Nebuchadnezzar king of Babylon, the Chaldean, *who* destroyed this temple and deported the people to Babylon. [13] 'However, in the first year of Cyrus king of Babylon, King Cyrus issued a decree to rebuild this house of God. [14] 'Also the gold and silver utensils of the house of God which Nebuchadnezzar had taken from the temple in Jerusalem, and brought them to the temple of Babylon, these King Cyrus took from the temple of Babylon and they were given to one whose name was Sheshbazzar, whom he had appointed governor. [15] 'He said to him, "Take these utensils, go *and* deposit them in the temple in Jerusalem and let the house of God be rebuilt in its place." [16] 'Then that Sheshbazzar came *and* laid the foundations of the house of God in Jerusalem; and from then until now it has been under construction and it is not *yet* completed.' [17] "Now if it pleases the king, let a search be conducted in the king's treasure house, which is there in Babylon, if it be that a decree was issued by King Cyrus to rebuild this house of God at Jerusalem; and let the king send to us his decision concerning this *matter*."

Discussion

This chapter documents a letter sent from Tattenai to Darius about rebuilding the Temple of the LORD in Jerusalem.

Biblical Personalities

1. Haggai – "Haggai (1:1) was a prophet who, along with Zechariah, encouraged the returned exiles to rebuild the temple (see Ezr 5:1-2; 6:14). Haggai means "festal," which may indicate that the prophet was born during one of the three pilgrimage feasts (Unleavened Bread, Pentecost or Weeks, and Tabernacles; cf. Dt 16:16). Based on 2:3 (see note there) Haggai may

have witnessed the destruction of Solomon's temple. If so, he must have been in his 70s during his ministry."[41]

2. Tattenai, "also called Sisinnes, (flourished *c.* 6th–5th century BCE), Persian governor of the province west of the Euphrates River (*eber nāri,* "beyond the river") during the reign of Darius I (522–486 BCE).

   According to the Hebrew Bible (Old Testament) Book of Ezra, Tattenai led an investigation into the rebuilding of the Temple in Jerusalem about 519 BCE. He sent a report to Darius, who responded with instructions to allow the work to proceed. Tattenai is one of the few Persian officials mentioned in the Hebrew Bible for whom there is independent attestation; he is mentioned in a cuneiform tablet dated 502 BCE."[42]

3. SHETHAR-BOZENAI "she' thär bŏz' ə nī (שְׁתַר בּוֹזְנַי; KJV SHETHAR-BOZNAI, shē' thär bŏz'-nī; cf. alternate in 1 Esdras 6:3, 7, 27; 7:1, SATHRABUZANES, săth' rə bū' ze nəz; Gr. Σαθραβουζάνης). A person associated with Tattenai, the governor of the province of Trans-Euphratia ("Beyond the River," located W of the Euphrates, which included Pal.). Shethar-Bozenai was numbered among the governor's staff, and may have been the official scribe who wrote a letter to Darius, the Pers. king, regarding the activity of the Jews who were rebuilding the Temple at Jerusalem. Darius returned a decree requiring them to refrain from

---

[41] BibleStudyTools Staff, "Book of Haggai - Read, Study Bible Verses Online," biblestudytools.com (BibleStudyTools, January 25, 2021), https://www.biblestudytools.com/haggai/.

[42] "Tattenai," Encyclopædia Britannica (Encyclopædia Britannica, inc.), accessed January 25, 2021, https://www.britannica.com/biography/Tattenai.

hindering, and to assist completion of the building, and its continuing services, in every way possible."[43]

Phrase Study

1. וְעֵין אֱלָהֲהֹם – means "and the eye of God." This means that the LORD knew exactly what was happening. The LORD knew that the Temple's rebuilding at Jerusalem had started and shown favor to the Israelites who worked on this project.

Thoughts

The LORD looked at the work of rebuilding His Temple at Jerusalem and was pleased. The letter was sent to Darius to document the work. The Persian king found favor with the LORD, and allowed Israel to return from Exile to rebuild the Temple was his way to express his thanksgiving.

---

[43] Shethar-Bozenai - Encyclopedia of The Bible - Bible Gateway, accessed January 25, 2021, https://www.biblegateway.com/resources/encyclopedia-of-the-bible/Shethar-Bozenai.

64

Chapter Six

Language

New American Standard 1995	Hebrew
[1] Then King Darius issued a decree, and search was made in the archives, where the treasures were stored in Babylon. [2] In Ecbatana in the fortress, which is in the province of Media, a scroll was found and there was written in it as follows: "Memorandum — [3] "In the first year of King Cyrus, Cyrus the king issued a decree: '*Concerning* the house of God at Jerusalem, let the temple, the place where sacrifices are offered, be rebuilt and let its foundations be retained, its height being 60 cubits and its width 60 cubits; [4] with three layers of huge stones and one layer of timbers. And let the cost be paid from the royal treasury. [5] 'Also let the gold and silver utensils of the house of God, which Nebuchadnezzar took from the temple in Jerusalem and brought to Babylon, be returned and brought to their places in the temple in Jerusalem; and you shall put *them* in the house of God.' [6] "Now *therefore,* Tattenai, governor of *the province* beyond the River, Shethar-bozenai and your colleagues, the officials of *the provinces* beyond the River, keep away from there. [7] "Leave this work on the house of God alone; let the governor of the Jews and the elders of the Jews rebuild this house of God on its site. [8] "Moreover, I issue a decree concerning what you are to do for these elders of Judah in the rebuilding of this house of	בֵּאדַיִן דָּרְיָוֶשׁ מַלְכָּא שָׂם טְעֵם וּבַקַּרוּ ׀ בְּבֵית סִפְרַיָּא דִּי גִנְזַיָּא מְהַחֲתִין תַּמָּה בְּבָבֶל ׃ [2] וְהִשְׁתְּכַח בְּאַחְמְתָא בְּבִירְתָא דִּי בְּמָדַי מְדִינְתָּה מְגִלָּה חֲדָה וְכֵן־ כְּתִיב בְּגַוַּהּ דִּכְרוֹנָה ׃ פ [3] בִּשְׁנַת חֲדָה לְכוֹרֶשׁ מַלְכָּא כּוֹרֶשׁ מַלְכָּא שָׂם טְעֵם בֵּית־אֱלָהָא בִירוּשְׁלֶם בַּיְתָא יִתְבְּנֵא אֲתַר דִּי־דָבְחִין דִּבְחִין וְאֻשּׁוֹהִי מְסוֹבְלִין רוּמֵהּ אַמִּין שִׁתִּין פְּתָיֵהּ אַמִּין שִׁתִּין ׃ [4] נִדְבָּכִין דִּי־אֶבֶן גְּלָל תְּלָתָא וְנִדְבָּךְ דִּי־אָע חֲדַת וְנִפְקְתָא מִן־בֵּית מַלְכָּא תִּתְיְהִב ׃ [5] וְאַף מָאנֵי בֵית־ אֱלָהָא דִּי דַהֲבָה וְכַסְפָּא דִּי נְבוּכַדְנֶצַּר הַנְפֵּק מִן־הֵיכְלָא דִי־בִירוּשְׁלֶם וְהֵיבֵל לְבָבֶל יַהֲתִיבוּן וִיהָךְ לְהֵיכְלָא דִי־ בִירוּשְׁלֶם לְאַתְרֵהּ וְתַחֵת בְּבֵית אֱלָהָא ׃ ס [6] כְּעַן תַּתְּנַי פַּחַת עֲבַר־נַהֲרָה שְׁתַר בּוֹזְנַי וּכְנָוָתְהוֹן אֲפַרְסְכָיֵא דִּי בַּעֲבַר נַהֲרָה רַחִיקִין הֲווֹ מִן־תַּמָּה ׃ [7] שְׁבֻקוּ לַעֲבִידַת בֵּית־אֱלָהָא דֵךְ פַּחַת יְהוּדָיֵא וּלְשָׂבֵי יְהוּדָיֵא בֵּית־אֱלָהָא דֵךְ יִבְנוֹן עַל־אַתְרֵהּ ׃ [8] וּמִנִּי שִׂים טְעֵם לְמָא דִּי־ תַעַבְדוּן עִם־שָׂבֵי יְהוּדָיֵא אִלֵּךְ לְמִבְנֵא בֵּית־אֱלָהָא דֵךְ וּמִנִּכְסֵי מַלְכָּא דִּי מִדַּת עֲבַר נַהֲרָה אָסְפַּרְנָא נִפְקְתָא

God: the full cost is to be paid to these people from the royal treasury out of the taxes of *the provinces* beyond the River, and that without delay. [9] "Whatever is needed, both young bulls, rams, and lambs for a burnt offering to the God of heaven, and wheat, salt, wine and anointing oil, as the priests in Jerusalem request, *it* is to be given to them daily without fail, [10] that they may offer acceptable sacrifices to the God of heaven and pray for the life of the king and his sons. [11] "And I issued a decree that any man who violates this edict, a timber shall be drawn from his house and he shall be impaled on it and his house shall be made a refuse heap on account of this. [12] "May the God who has caused His name to dwell there overthrow any king or people who attempts to change *it,* so as to destroy this house of God in Jerusalem. I, Darius, have issued *this* decree, let *it* be carried out with all diligence!" [13] Then Tattenai, the governor of *the province* beyond the River, Shethar-bozenai and their colleagues carried out *the decree* with all diligence, just as King Darius had sent. [14] And the elders of the Jews [1]were successful in building through the prophesying of Haggai the prophet and Zechariah the son of Iddo. And they finished building according to the command of the God of Israel and the decree of Cyrus, Darius, and Artaxerxes king of Persia. [15] This temple was completed on the third day of the month Adar; it was the sixth year of the reign of King Darius. [16] And the sons of Israel, the priests, the Levites and the rest of the exiles, celebrated the dedication of this house of God with joy. [17] They

תֶּהֱוֵא מִתְיַהֲבָא לְגֻבְרַיָּא אִלֵּךְ דִּי־לָא
לְבַטָּלָא ׃ 9 וּמָה חַשְׁחָן וּבְנֵי תוֹרִין
וְדִכְרִין וְאִמְּרִין לַעֲלָוָן לֶאֱלָהּ שְׁמַיָּא
חִנְטִין מְלַח ׀ חֲמַר וּמְשַׁח כְּמֵאמַר
כָּהֲנַיָּא דִי־בִירוּשְׁלֶם לֶהֱוֵא מִתְיְהֵב
לְהֹם יוֹם ׀ בְּיוֹם דִּי־לָא שָׁלוּ ׃ 10 דִּי־
לֶהֱוֹן מְהַקְרְבִין נִיחוֹחִין לֶאֱלָהּ שְׁמַיָּא
וּמְצַלַּיִן לְחַיֵּי מַלְכָּא וּבְנוֹהִי ׃ 11 וּמִנִּי
שִׂים טְעֵם דִּי כָל־אֱנָשׁ דִּי יְהַשְׁנֵא
פִּתְגָמָא דְנָה יִתְנְסַח אָע מִן־בַּיְתֵהּ
וּזְקִיף יִתְמְחֵא עֲלֹהִי וּבַיְתֵהּ נְוָלוּ
יִתְעֲבֵד עַל־דְּנָה ׃ 12 וֵאלָהָא דִּי שַׁכֵּן
שְׁמֵהּ תַּמָּה יְמַגַּר כָּל־מֶלֶךְ וְעַם דִּי ׀
יִשְׁלַח יְדֵהּ לְהַשְׁנָיָה לְחַבָּלָה בֵּית־
אֱלָהָא דֵךְ דִּי בִירוּשְׁלֶם אֲנָה דָרְיָוֶשׁ
שָׂמֵת טְעֵם אָסְפַּרְנָא יִתְעֲבִד ׃ פ 13
אֱדַיִן תַּתְּנַי פַּחַת עֲבַר־נַהֲרָה שְׁתַר
בּוֹזְנַי וּכְנָוָתְהוֹן לָקֳבֵל דִּי־שְׁלַח דָּרְיָוֶשׁ
מַלְכָּא כְּנֵמָא אָסְפַּרְנָא עֲבַדוּ ׃ 14 וְשָׂבֵי
יְהוּדָיֵא בָּנַיִן וּמַצְלְחִין בִּנְבוּאַת חַגַּי
נְבִיָּאה [נְבִיָּ֗א] וּזְכַרְיָה בַּר־עִדּוֹא
וּבְנוֹ וְשַׁכְלִלוּ מִן־טַעַם אֱלָהּ יִשְׂרָאֵל
וּמִטְּעֵם כּוֹרֶשׁ וְדָרְיָוֶשׁ וְאַרְתַּחְשַׁשְׂתְּא
מֶלֶךְ פָּרָס ׃ 15 וְשֵׁיצִיא בַּיְתָה דְנָה עַד
יוֹם תְּלָתָה לִירַח אֲדָר דִּי־הִיא שְׁנַת־
שֵׁת לְמַלְכוּת דָּרְיָוֶשׁ מַלְכָּא ׃ פ 16
וַעֲבַדוּ בְנֵי־יִשְׂרָאֵל כָּהֲנַיָּא וְלֵוָיֵא וּשְׁאָר
בְּנֵי־גָלוּתָא חֲנֻכַּת בֵּית־אֱלָהָא דְנָה
בְּחֶדְוָה ׃ 17 וְהַקְרִבוּ לַחֲנֻכַּת בֵּית־
אֱלָהָא דְנָה תּוֹרִין מְאָה דִּכְרִין מָאתַיִן
אִמְּרִין אַרְבַּע מְאָה וּצְפִירֵי עִזִּין

offered for the dedication of this temple of God 100 bulls, 200 rams, 400 lambs, and as a sin offering for all Israel 12 male goats, corresponding to the number of the tribes of Israel. [18] Then they appointed the priests to their divisions and the Levites in their orders for the service of God in Jerusalem, as it is written in the book of Moses. [19] The exiles observed the Passover on the fourteenth of the first month. [20] For the priests and the Levites had purified themselves together; all of them were pure. Then they slaughtered the Passover *lamb* for all the exiles, both for their brothers the priests and for themselves. [21] The sons of Israel who returned from exile and all those who had separated themselves from the impurity of the nations of the land to *join* them, to seek the LORD God of Israel, ate *the Passover.* [22] And they observed the Feast of Unleavened Bread seven days with joy, for the LORD had caused them to rejoice, and had turned the heart of ʿthe king of Assyria toward them to encourage them in the work of the house of God, the God of Israel.

לְחַטָּיָא [ל][חַטָּאָה] עַל־כָּל־יִשְׂרָאֵל
תְּרֵי־עֲשַׂר לְמִנְיָן שִׁבְטֵי יִשְׂרָאֵל׃ 18
וַהֲקִימוּ כָהֲנַיָּא בִּפְלֻגָּתְהוֹן וְלֵוָיֵא
בְּמַחְלְקָתְהוֹן עַל־עֲבִידַת אֱלָהָא דִּי
בִירוּשְׁלֶם כִּכְתָב סְפַר מֹשֶׁה׃ פ 19
וַיַּעֲשׂוּ בְנֵי־הַגּוֹלָה אֶת־הַפָּסַח בְּאַרְבָּעָה
עָשָׂר לַחֹדֶשׁ הָרִאשׁוֹן׃ 20 כִּי הִטַּהֲרוּ
הַכֹּהֲנִים וְהַלְוִיִּם כְּאֶחָד כֻּלָּם טְהוֹרִים
וַיִּשְׁחֲטוּ הַפֶּסַח לְכָל־בְּנֵי הַגּוֹלָה
וְלַאֲחֵיהֶם הַכֹּהֲנִים וְלָהֶם׃ 21 וַיֹּאכְלוּ
בְנֵי־יִשְׂרָאֵל הַשָּׁבִים מֵהַגּוֹלָה וְכֹל
הַנִּבְדָּל מִטֻּמְאַת גּוֹיֵ־הָאָרֶץ אֲלֵהֶם
לִדְרֹשׁ לַיהוָה אֱלֹהֵי יִשְׂרָאֵל׃ 22 וַיַּעֲשׂוּ
חַג־מַצּוֹת שִׁבְעַת יָמִים בְּשִׂמְחָה כִּי ׀
שִׂמְּחָם יְהוָה וְהֵסֵב לֵב מֶלֶךְ־אַשּׁוּר
עֲלֵיהֶם לְחַזֵּק יְדֵיהֶם בִּמְלֶאכֶת בֵּית־
הָאֱלֹהִים אֱלֹהֵי יִשְׂרָאֵל׃ פ

Process of Discovery

Linguistics Section

Linguistic Structure

[Transition] [1] Then King Darius issued a decree, and search was made in the archives, where the treasures were stored in Babylon.

[Letter of Cyrus] [2] In Ecbatana in the fortress, which is in the province of Media, a scroll was found and there was written in it as follows: "Memorandum — [3] "In the first year of King Cyrus, Cyrus the king issued a decree: '*Concerning* the house of God at Jerusalem, let the temple, the place where sacrifices are offered, be rebuilt and let its foundations be retained, its height being 60 cubits and its width 60 cubits; [4] with three layers of huge stones and one layer of timbers. And let the cost be paid from the royal treasury. [5] 'Also let the gold and silver utensils of the house of God, which Nebuchadnezzar took from the temple in Jerusalem and brought to Babylon, be returned and brought to their places in the temple in Jerusalem; and you shall put *them* in the house of God.' [6] "Now *therefore,* Tattenai, governor of *the province* beyond the River, Shethar-bozenai and your colleagues, the officials of *the provinces* beyond the River, keep away from there. [7] "Leave this work on the house of God alone; let the governor of the Jews and the elders of the Jews rebuild this house of God on its site. [8] "Moreover, I issue a decree concerning what you are to do for these elders of Judah in the rebuilding of this house of God: the full cost is to be paid to these people from the royal treasury out of the taxes of *the provinces* beyond the River, and that without delay. [9] "Whatever is needed, both young bulls, rams, and lambs for a burnt offering to the God of heaven, and wheat, salt, wine and anointing oil, as the priests in Jerusalem request, *it* is to be given to them daily without fail, [10] that they may offer acceptable sacrifices to the God of heaven and pray for the life of the king and his sons. [11] "And I issued a decree that any man who violates this edict, a timber shall be drawn from his house and he shall be impaled on it and his house shall be made a refuse heap on account of this. [12] "May the God who has caused His name to dwell there overthrow any king or people who attempts to change *it,* so as to destroy this house of God in Jerusalem. I, Darius, have issued *this* decree, let *it* be carried out with all diligence!"

[Temple Completion] [13]   Then Tattenai, the governor of *the province* beyond the River, Shethar-bozenai and their colleagues carried out *the decree* with all diligence, just as King Darius had sent. [14] And the elders of the Jews [1]were successful in building through the prophesying of Haggai the prophet and Zechariah the son of Iddo. And they finished building according to the command of the God of Israel and the decree of Cyrus, Darius, and Artaxerxes king of Persia. [15] This temple was completed on the third day of the month Adar; it was the sixth year of the reign of King Darius.

[Temple Completion Celebration] [16] And the sons of Israel, the priests, the Levites and the rest of the exiles, celebrated the dedication of this house of God with joy. [17] They offered for the dedication of this temple of God 100 bulls, 200 rams, 400 lambs, and as a sin offering for all Israel 12 male goats, corresponding to the number of the tribes of Israel. [18] Then they appointed the priests to their divisions and the Levites in their orders for the service of God in Jerusalem, as it is written in the book of Moses. [19] The exiles observed the Passover on the fourteenth of the first month. [20] For the priests and the Levites had purified themselves together; all of them were pure. Then they slaughtered the Passover *lamb* for all the exiles, both for their brothers the priests and for themselves. [21] The sons of Israel who returned from exile and all those who had separated themselves from the impurity of the nations of the land to *join* them, to seek the LORD God of Israel, ate *the Passover.* [22] And they observed the Feast of Unleavened Bread seven days with joy, for the LORD had caused them to rejoice, and had turned the heart of 'the king of Assyria toward them to encourage them in the work of the house of God, the God of Israel.

Discussion

This chapter has the letter from Cyrus about the rebuilding of the temple and its completion.

Questioning the Passage

1. What is the date of the completion of the Second Temple? (v. 15)

   Adar 3rd was in the year 516 BCE.

Culture Section

Questioning the passage

1. What is the penalty described in verse eleven?

   The punishment was crucifixion. This method was a form of punishment created by the Assyrians and was used in the Babylonian and Persian Empires.

Thoughts

The Second Temple in Jerusalem was completed in 516 BCE. The center of Judaism had been restored. The enormous sacrifice to celebrate the completion of the project says that a massive feast was held. There would have been a large number of workers and Jerusalem city dwellers who participated in the celebration. It is a good thing to hold a celebration when a project dedicated to the LORD is completed.

Chapter Seven

Language

New American Standard 1995	Hebrew
[1] Now after these things, in the reign of Artaxerxes king of Persia, *there went up* Ezra son of Seraiah, son of Azariah, son of Hilkiah, (Ezr. 7:1 NAU) [2] son of Shallum, son of Zadok, son of Ahitub, [3] son of Amariah, son of Azariah, son of Meraioth, [4] son of Zerahiah, son of Uzzi, son of Bukki, [5] son of Abishua, son of Phinehas, son of Eleazar, son of Aaron the chief priest. [6] This Ezra went up from Babylon, and he was a scribe skilled in the law of Moses, which the LORD God of Israel had given; and the king granted him all he requested because the hand of the LORD his God *was* upon him. [7] Some of the sons of Israel and some of the priests, the Levites, the singers, the gatekeepers and the temple servants went up to Jerusalem in the seventh year of King Artaxerxes. [8] He came to Jerusalem in the fifth month, which was in the seventh year of the king. [9] For on the first of the first month he began to go up from Babylon; and on the first of the fifth month he came to Jerusalem, because the good hand of his God *was* upon him. [10] For Ezra had set his heart to study the law of the LORD and to practice *it*, and to teach *His* statutes and ordinances in Israel.	וְאַחַר הַדְּבָרִים הָאֵלֶּה בְּמַלְכוּת אַרְתַּחְשַׁסְתְּא מֶלֶךְ־פָּרָס עֶזְרָא בֶּן־שְׂרָיָה בֶּן־עֲזַרְיָה בֶּן־חִלְקִיָּה: [2] בֶּן־שַׁלּוּם בֶּן־צָדוֹק בֶּן־אֲחִיטוּב: [3] בֶּן־אֲמַרְיָה בֶן־עֲזַרְיָה בֶּן־מְרָיוֹת: [4] בֶּן־זְרַחְיָה בֶן־עֻזִּי בֶּן־בֻּקִּי: [5] בֶּן־אֲבִישׁוּעַ בֶּן־פִּינְחָס בֶּן־אֶלְעָזָר בֶּן־אַהֲרֹן הַכֹּהֵן הָרֹאשׁ: [6] הוּא עֶזְרָא עָלָה מִבָּבֶל וְהוּא־סֹפֵר מָהִיר בְּתוֹרַת מֹשֶׁה אֲשֶׁר־נָתַן יְהוָה אֱלֹהֵי יִשְׂרָאֵל וַיִּתֶּן־לוֹ הַמֶּלֶךְ כְּיַד־יְהוָה אֱלֹהָיו עָלָיו כֹּל בַּקָּשָׁתוֹ: פ [7] וַיַּעֲלוּ מִבְּנֵי־יִשְׂרָאֵל וּמִן־הַכֹּהֲנִים וְהַלְוִיִּם וְהַמְשֹׁרְרִים וְהַשֹּׁעֲרִים וְהַנְּתִינִים אֶל־יְרוּשָׁלִָם בִּשְׁנַת־שֶׁבַע לְאַרְתַּחְשַׁסְתְּא הַמֶּלֶךְ: [8] וַיָּבֹא יְרוּשָׁלִַם בַּחֹדֶשׁ הַחֲמִישִׁי הִיא שְׁנַת הַשְּׁבִיעִית לַמֶּלֶךְ: [9] כִּי בְּאֶחָד לַחֹדֶשׁ הָרִאשׁוֹן הוּא יְסֻד הַמַּעֲלָה מִבָּבֶל וּבְאֶחָד לַחֹדֶשׁ הַחֲמִישִׁי בָּא אֶל־יְרוּשָׁלִַם כְּיַד־אֱלֹהָיו הַטּוֹבָה עָלָיו: [10] כִּי עֶזְרָא הֵכִין לְבָבוֹ לִדְרוֹשׁ אֶת־תּוֹרַת יְהוָה וְלַעֲשֹׂת וּלְלַמֵּד בְּיִשְׂרָאֵל חֹק וּמִשְׁפָּט: ס [11] וְזֶה פַּרְשֶׁגֶן הַנִּשְׁתְּוָן אֲשֶׁר נָתַן הַמֶּלֶךְ אַרְתַּחְשַׁסְתְּא לְעֶזְרָא הַכֹּהֵן הַסֹּפֵר סֹפֵר דִּבְרֵי מִצְוֹת־יְהוָה וְחֻקָּיו עַל־יִשְׂרָאֵל: פ

¹¹ Now this is the copy of the decree which King Artaxerxes gave to Ezra the priest, the scribe, learned in the words of the commandments of the LORD and His statutes to Israel:

¹² "Artaxerxes, king of kings, to Ezra the priest, the scribe of the law of the God of heaven, perfect *peace*. And now

¹³ I have issued a decree that any of the people of Israel and their priests and the Levites in my kingdom who are willing to go to Jerusalem, may go with you.

¹⁴ "Forasmuch as you are sent by the king and his seven counselors to inquire concerning Judah and Jerusalem according to the law of your God which is in your hand,

¹⁵ and to bring the silver and gold, which the king and his counselors have freely offered to the God of Israel, whose dwelling is in Jerusalem,

¹⁶ with all the silver and gold which you find in the whole province of Babylon, along with the freewill offering of the people and of the priests, who offered willingly for the house of their God which is in Jerusalem;

¹⁷ with this money, therefore, you shall diligently buy bulls, rams and lambs, with their grain offerings and their drink offerings and offer them on the altar of the house of your God which is in Jerusalem.

¹⁸ "Whatever seems good to you and to your brothers to do with the rest of the silver and gold, you may do according to the will of your God.

¹⁹ "Also the utensils which are given to you for the service of the house of your

אַרְתַּחְשַׁסְתְּא מֶלֶךְ מַלְכַיָּא לְעֶזְרָא ¹²
כָהֲנָא סָפַר דָּתָא דִּי־אֱלָהּ שְׁמַיָּא גְּמִיר
וּכְעֶנֶת:

מִנִּי שִׂים טְעֵם דִּי כָל־מִתְנַדַּב ¹³
בְּמַלְכוּתִי מִן־עַמָּה יִשְׂרָאֵל וְכָהֲנוֹהִי
וְלֵוָיֵא לִמְהָךְ לִירוּשְׁלֶם עִמָּךְ יְהָךְ:

כָּל־קֳבֵל דִּי מִן־קֳדָם מַלְכָּא וְשִׁבְעַת ¹⁴
יָעֲטֹהִי שְׁלִיחַ לְבַקָּרָא עַל־יְהוּד
וְלִירוּשְׁלֶם בְּדָת אֱלָהָךְ דִּי בִידָךְ:

וּלְהֵיבָלָה כְּסַף וּדְהַב דִּי־מַלְכָּא ¹⁵
וְיָעֲטוֹהִי הִתְנַדַּבוּ לֶאֱלָהּ יִשְׂרָאֵל דִּי
בִירוּשְׁלֶם מִשְׁכְּנֵהּ:

וְכֹל כְּסַף וּדְהַב דִּי תְהַשְׁכַּח בְּכֹל ¹⁶
מְדִינַת בָּבֶל עִם הִתְנַדָּבוּת עַמָּא
וְכָהֲנַיָּא מִתְנַדְּבִין לְבֵית אֱלָהֲהֹם דִּי
בִירוּשְׁלֶם:

כָּל־קֳבֵל דְּנָה אָסְפַּרְנָא תִּקְנֵא ¹⁷
בְּכַסְפָּא דְנָה תּוֹרִין דִּכְרִין אִמְּרִין
וּמִנְחָתְהוֹן וְנִסְכֵּיהוֹן וּתְקָרֵב הִמּוֹ עַל־
מַדְבְּחָה דִּי בֵּית אֱלָהֲכֹם דִּי בִירוּשְׁלֶם:

וּמָה דִי (עֲלַיִךְ) [עֲלָךְ] וְעַל־(אֶחַיִךְ) ¹⁸
[אֶחָךְ] יֵיטַב בִּשְׁאָר כַּסְפָּא וְדַהֲבָה
לְמֶעְבַּד כִּרְעוּת אֱלָהֲכֹם תַּעַבְדוּן:

וּמָאנַיָּא דִּי־מִתְיַהֲבִין לָךְ לְפָלְחָן בֵּית ¹⁹
אֱלָהָךְ הַשְׁלֵם קֳדָם אֱלָהּ יְרוּשְׁלֶם:

וּשְׁאָר חַשְׁחוּת בֵּית אֱלָהָךְ דִּי יִפֶּל־ ²⁰
לָךְ לְמִנְתַּן תִּנְתֵּן מִן־בֵּית גִּנְזֵי מַלְכָּא:

וּמִנִּי אֲנָה אַרְתַּחְשַׁסְתְּא מַלְכָּא שִׂים ²¹
טְעֵם לְכֹל גִּזַּבְרַיָּא דִּי בַּעֲבַר נַהֲרָה דִּי
כָל־דִּי יִשְׁאֲלֶנְכוֹן עֶזְרָא כָהֲנָה סָפַר
דָּתָא דִּי־אֱלָהּ שְׁמַיָּא אָסְפַּרְנָא יִתְעֲבִד:

עַד־כְּסַף כַּכְּרִין מְאָה וְעַד־חִנְטִין ²²
כֹּרִין מְאָה וְעַד־חֲמַר בַּתִּין מְאָה וְעַד־
בַּתִּין מְשַׁח מְאָה וּמְלַח דִּי־לָא כְתָב:

God, deliver in full before the God of Jerusalem.

20 "The rest of the needs for the house of your God, for which you may have occasion to provide, provide *for it* from the royal treasury.

21 "I, even I, King Artaxerxes, issue a decree to all the treasurers who are *in the provinces* beyond the River, that whatever Ezra the priest, the scribe of the law of the God of heaven, may require of you, it shall be done diligently,

22 *even* up to 100 talents of silver, 100 kors of wheat, 100 baths of wine, 100 baths of oil, and salt as needed.

23 "Whatever is commanded by the God of heaven, let it be done with zeal for the house of the God of heaven, so that there will not be wrath against the kingdom of the king and his sons.

24 "We also inform you that it is not allowed to impose tax, tribute or toll *on* any of the priests, Levites, singers, doorkeepers, Nethinim or servants of this house of God.

25 "You, Ezra, according to the wisdom of your God which is in your hand, appoint magistrates and judges that they may judge all the people who are in *the province* beyond the River, *even* all those who know the laws of your God; and you may teach anyone who is ignorant *of them.*

26 "Whoever will not observe the law of your God and the law of the king, let judgment be executed upon him strictly, whether for death or for banishment or for confiscation of goods or for imprisonment."

27 Blessed be the LORD, the God of our fathers, who has put *such a thing* as this in

23 כָּל־דִּי מִן־טַעַם אֱלָהּ שְׁמַיָּא יִתְעֲבֵד אַדְרַזְדָּא לְבֵית אֱלָהּ שְׁמַיָּא דִּי־לְמָה לֶהֱוֵא קְצַף עַל־מַלְכוּת מַלְכָּא וּבְנוֹהִי:

24 וּלְכֹם מְהוֹדְעִין דִּי כָל־כָּהֲנַיָּא וְלֵוָיֵא זַמָּרַיָּא תָרָעַיָּא נְתִינַיָּא וּפָלְחֵי בֵּית אֱלָהָא דְנָה מִנְדָּה בְלוֹ וַהֲלָךְ לָא שַׁלִּיט לְמִרְמֵא עֲלֵיהֹם:

25 וְאַנְתְּ עֶזְרָא כְּחָכְמַת אֱלָהָךְ דִּי־בִידָךְ מֶנִּי שָׁפְטִין וְדַיָּנִין דִּי־לֶהֱוֹן (דָּאנִין) [דָּאיְנִין] לְכָל־עַמָּה דִּי בַּעֲבַר נַהֲרָה לְכָל־יָדְעֵי דָּתֵי אֱלָהָךְ וְדִי לָ_א יָדַע תְּהוֹדְעוּן:

26 וְכָל־דִּי־לָא לֶהֱוֵא עָבֵד דָּתָא דִי־אֱלָהָךְ וְדָתָא דִּי מַלְכָּא אָסְפַּרְנָא דִּינָה לֶהֱוֵא מִתְעֲבֵד מִנֵּהּ הֵן לְמוֹת הֵן (לִשְׁרֹשׁוּ) [לִשְׁרֹשִׁי] הֵן־לַעֲנָשׁ נִכְסִין וְלֶאֱסוּרִין: פ

27 בָּרוּךְ יְהוָה אֱלֹהֵי אֲבוֹתֵינוּ אֲשֶׁר נָתַן כָּזֹאת בְּלֵב הַמֶּלֶךְ לְפָאֵר אֶת־בֵּית יְהוָה אֲשֶׁר בִּירוּשָׁלָםִ:

28 וְעָלַי הִטָּה־חֶסֶד לִפְנֵי הַמֶּלֶךְ וְיוֹעֲצָיו וּלְכָל־שָׂרֵי הַמֶּלֶךְ הַגִּבֹּרִים וַאֲנִי הִתְחַזַּקְתִּי כְּיַד־יְהוָה אֱלֹהַי עָלַי וָאֶקְבְּצָה מִיִּשְׂרָאֵל רָאשִׁים לַעֲלוֹת עִמִּי: פ

the king's heart, to adorn the house of the LORD which is in Jerusalem, [28] and has extended lovingkindness to me before the king and his counselors and before all the king's mighty princes. Thus I was strengthened according to the hand of the LORD my God upon me, and I gathered leading men from Israel to go up with me.	

Process of Discovery

Linguistics Section

Linguistic Structure

[Who was Ezra?] [1] Now after these things, in the reign of Artaxerxes king of Persia, *there went up* Ezra son of Seraiah, son of Azariah, son of Hilkiah, [2] son of Shallum, son of Zadok, son of Ahitub, [3] son of Amariah, son of Azariah, son of Meraioth, [4] son of Zerahiah, son of Uzzi, son of Bukki, [5] son of Abishua, son of Phinehas, son of Eleazar, son of Aaron the chief priest. [6] This Ezra went up from Babylon, and he was a scribe skilled in the law of Moses, which the LORD God of Israel had given; and the king granted him all he requested because the hand of the LORD his God *was* upon him. [7] Some of the sons of Israel and some of the priests, the Levites, the singers, the gatekeepers and the temple servants went up to Jerusalem in the seventh year of King Artaxerxes. [8] He came to Jerusalem in the fifth month, which was in the seventh year of the king. [9] For on the first of the first month he began to go up from Babylon; and on the first of the fifth month he came to Jerusalem, because the good hand of his God *was* upon him. [10] For Ezra had set his heart to study the law of the LORD and to practice *it*, and to teach *His* statutes and ordinances in Israel.

[Artaxerxes letter to Ezra] [11] Now this is the copy of the decree which King Artaxerxes gave to Ezra the priest, the scribe, learned in the words of the commandments of the LORD and His statutes to Israel: [12] "Artaxerxes, king of kings, to Ezra the priest, the scribe of the law of the God of heaven, perfect *peace*. And now [13] I have issued a decree that any of the people of Israel and their priests and the Levites in my kingdom who are willing to go to Jerusalem, may go with you. [14] "Forasmuch as you are sent by the king and his seven counselors to inquire concerning Judah and Jerusalem according to the law of your God which is in your hand, [15] and to bring the silver and gold, which the king and his counselors have freely offered to the God of Israel, whose dwelling is in Jerusalem, [16] with all the silver and gold which you find in the whole province of Babylon, along with the freewill offering of the people and of the priests, who offered willingly for the house of their God which is in Jerusalem; [17] with this money, therefore, you shall diligently buy bulls, rams and lambs, with their grain offerings and their drink offerings and offer them on the altar of the house of your God which is in Jerusalem. [18] "Whatever seems good to you and to your brothers to do with the rest of the silver and gold, you may do according to the will of your God. [19] "Also the utensils which are given to you for the service of the house of your God, deliver in full before the God of Jerusalem. [20] "The rest of the needs for the house of your God, for which you may have occasion to provide, provide *for it* from the royal treasury. [21] "I, even I, King Artaxerxes, issue a decree to all the treasurers who are *in the provinces* beyond the River, that whatever Ezra the priest, the scribe of the law of the God of heaven, may require of you, it shall be done diligently, [22] *even* up to 100 talents of silver, 100 kors of wheat, 100 baths of wine, 100 baths of oil, and salt as needed. [23] "Whatever is commanded by the God of heaven, let it be done with zeal for the house of the God of heaven, so that there will not be wrath against the kingdom of the king and his sons. [24] "We also inform you that it is not allowed to impose tax, tribute or toll *on* any of the priests, Levites, singers, doorkeepers, Nethinim or servants of this house of God. [25] "You, Ezra, according to the wisdom of your God which is in your hand, appoint magistrates and judges that they may judge all the people who are in *the province* beyond the River, *even* all those who know the laws of your God; and you may teach anyone who is ignorant *of them.* [26] "Whoever will not observe the law of your God and the law of the king, let judgment be executed upon him strictly, whether for death or for banishment or for confiscation of goods or for imprisonment." [27] Blessed be the LORD, the God of our fathers, who has put *such a thing* as this in the king's heart, to adorn the house of the LORD which is in Jerusalem, [28] and has extended lovingkindness to me before the king and his counselors and before all the king's mighty princes. Thus I was strengthened according to the hand of the LORD my God upon me, and I gathered leading men from Israel to go up with me.

Discussion

This chapter tells the reader who Ezra was. It also contains a letter from King Artaxerxes to Ezra about the need to build the Temple in Jerusalem and how it was paid for.

Questioning the Passage

1. What year was the seventh year of King Artaxerxes? (v. 7)

   458 BCE.

2. What are talents in pounds? (v. 22)

   75 pounds equals one talent.

3. How much wheat is a kor? (v. 22)

   15 bushels.

4. How much is a bath of wine or oil? (v. 22)

   8.7 gallons

Biblical Personalities

1. Who were the Nethinim? (v. 24)

   "The name given to the hereditary temple servants in all the post-Exilian books of Scripture. The word means given, i.e., "those set apart", viz., to the menial work of the sanctuary for the Levites. The name occurs seventeen times, and in each case in the Authorized Version incorrectly terminates in "s", "Nethinims;" in the Revised Version, correctly without the "s" (Ezra 2:70 ; Ezra 7:7 Ezra 7:24 ; 8:20 , etc.). The tradition is that the Gibeonites (Joshua 9:27) were the original caste, afterwards called Nethinim. Their numbers were added to afterwards from captives taken in battle; and they were formally given by David to the Levites (Ezra 8:20), and so were called Nethinim, i.e., the given ones, given to the Levites to be their servants. Only 612Nethinim returned from Babylon (Ezra 2:58 ; 8:20). They were under the control of a chief from among themselves (2:43 ; Nehemiah 7:46). No reference to them appears in the New Testament, because it is probable that they became merged in the general body of the Jewish people."[44]

Thoughts

The letter from King Artaxerxes clarified that the Temple's rebuilding at Jerusalem was to receive full support from the government. This promise included financial support. Anyone who tried to stop the work would be executed.

---

[44] "Nethinim Definition and Meaning - Bible Dictionary," biblestudytools.com, accessed January 29, 2021, https://www.biblestudytools.com/dictionary/nethinim/.

Chapter Eight

Language

New American Standard 1995	Hebrew
[1] Now these are the heads of their fathers' *households* and the genealogical enrollment of those who went up with me from Babylon in the reign of King Artaxerxes: [2] of the sons of Phinehas, Gershom; of the sons of Ithamar, Daniel; of the sons of David, Hattush; [3] of the sons of Shecaniah *who was* of the sons of Parosh, Zechariah and with him 150 males *who were in* the genealogical list; [4] of the sons of Pahath-moab, Eliehoenai the son of Zerahiah and 200 males with him; [5] of the sons of Zattu, Shecaniah, the son of Jahaziel and 300 males with him; [6] and of the sons of Adin, Ebed the son of Jonathan and 50 males with him; [7] and of the sons of Elam, Jeshaiah the son of Athaliah and 70 males with him; [8] and of the sons of Shephatiah, Zebadiah the son of Michael and 80 males with him; [9] of the sons of Joab, Obadiah the son of Jehiel and 218 males with him; [10] and of the sons of Bani, Shelomith, the son of Josiphiah and 160 males with him; [11] and of the sons of Bebai, Zechariah the son of Bebai and 28 males with him; [12] and of the sons of Azgad, Johanan the son of Hakkatan and 110 males with him; [13] and of the sons of Adonikam, the last ones, these being their names, Eliphelet, Jeuel and Shemaiah, and 60 males with them;	וְאֵ֛לֶּה רָאשֵׁ֥י אֲבֹתֵיהֶ֖ם וְהִתְיַחְשָׂ֑ם הָעֹלִ֣ים עִמִּ֗י בְּמַלְכ֛וּת אַרְתַּחְשַׁסְתְּ֥א הַמֶּ֖לֶךְ מִבָּבֶֽל׃ ס [2] מִבְּנֵ֤י פִֽינְחָס֙ גֵּֽרְשֹׁ֔ם ס מִבְּנֵ֥י אִֽיתָמָ֖ר דָּנִיֵּ֑אל ס מִבְּנֵ֥י דָוִ֖יד חַטּֽוּשׁ׃ ס [3] מִבְּנֵ֣י שְׁכַנְיָ֔ה ס מִבְּנֵ֥י פַרְעֹ֖שׁ זְכַרְיָ֑ה וְעִמּ֛וֹ הִתְיַחֵ֥שׂ לִזְכָרִ֖ים מֵאָ֥ה וַחֲמִשִּֽׁים׃ ס [4] מִבְּנֵי֙ פַּחַ֣ת מוֹאָ֔ב אֶלְיְהֽוֹעֵינַ֖י בֶּן־זְרַחְיָ֑ה וְעִמּ֖וֹ מָאתַ֥יִם הַזְּכָרִֽים׃ ס [5] מִבְּנֵ֣י שְׁכַנְיָ֔ה בֶּן־יַחֲזִיאֵ֑ל וְעִמּ֕וֹ שְׁלֹ֥שׁ מֵא֖וֹת הַזְּכָרִֽים׃ ס [6] וּמִבְּנֵ֣י עָדִ֔ין עֶ֥בֶד בֶּן־יוֹנָתָ֑ן וְעִמּ֖וֹ חֲמִשִּׁ֥ים הַזְּכָרִֽים׃ ס [7] וּמִבְּנֵ֣י עֵילָ֔ם יְשַֽׁעְיָ֖ה בֶּן־עֲתַלְיָ֑ה וְעִמּ֖וֹ שִׁבְעִ֥ים הַזְּכָרִֽים׃ ס [8] וּמִבְּנֵ֣י שְׁפַטְיָ֔ה זְבַדְיָ֖ה בֶּן־מִֽיכָאֵ֑ל וְעִמּ֖וֹ שְׁמֹנִ֥ים הַזְּכָרִֽים׃ ס [9] מִבְּנֵ֣י יוֹאָ֔ב עֹבַדְיָ֖ה בֶּן־יְחִיאֵ֑ל וְעִמּ֕וֹ מָאתַ֛יִם וּשְׁמֹנָ֥ה עָשָׂ֖ר הַזְּכָרִֽים׃ ס [10] וּמִבְּנֵ֣י שְׁלוֹמִ֔ית בֶּן־יוֹסִפְיָ֑ה וְעִמּ֕וֹ מֵאָ֥ה וְשִׁשִּׁ֖ים הַזְּכָרִֽים׃ ס [11] וּמִבְּנֵ֣י בֵבַ֔י זְכַרְיָ֖ה בֶּן־בֵּבָ֑י וְעִמּ֕וֹ עֶשְׂרִ֥ים וּשְׁמֹנָ֖ה הַזְּכָרִֽים׃ ס [12] וּמִבְּנֵ֣י עַזְגָּ֔ד יֽוֹחָנָ֖ן בֶּן־הַקָּטָ֑ן וְעִמּ֕וֹ מֵאָ֥ה וַעֲשָׂרָ֖ה הַזְּכָרִֽים׃ ס [13] וּמִבְּנֵ֣י אֲדֹנִיקָם֮ אַחֲרֹנִים֒ וְאֵ֣לֶּה שְׁמוֹתָ֔ם אֱלִיפֶ֖לֶט יְעִיאֵ֣ל וּֽשְׁמַֽעְיָ֑ה וְעִמָּהֶ֖ם שִׁשִּׁ֥ים הַזְּכָרִֽים׃ ס [14] וּמִבְּנֵ֥י בִגְוַ֖י עוּתַ֣י (וְזָב֑וּד) [וְזַכּ֑וּר] וְעִמּ֖וֹ שִׁבְעִ֥ים הַזְּכָרִֽים׃ פ [15] וָֽאֶקְבְּצֵ֗ם אֶל־הַנָּהָר֙ הַבָּ֣א אֶֽל־אַהֲוָ֔א וַנַּחֲנֶ֥ה שָׁ֖ם יָמִ֣ים שְׁלֹשָׁ֑ה וָאָבִ֤ינָה בָעָם֙ וּבַכֹּ֣הֲנִ֔ים וּמִבְּנֵ֥י לֵוִ֖י לֹא־מָצָ֥אתִי שָֽׁם׃

¹⁴ and of the sons of Bigvai, Uthai and Zabbud, and 70 males with them.

¹⁵ Now I assembled them at the river that runs to Ahava, where we camped for three days; and when I observed the people and the priests, I did not find any Levites there.

¹⁶ So I sent for Eliezer, Ariel, Shemaiah, Elnathan, Jarib, Elnathan, Nathan, Zechariah and Meshullam, leading men, and for Joiarib and Elnathan, teachers.

¹⁷ I sent them to Iddo the leading man at the place Casiphia; and I told them what to say to Iddo *and* his brothers, the temple servants at the place Casiphia, *that is*, to bring ministers to us for the house of our God.

¹⁸ According to the good hand of our God upon us they brought us a man of insight of the sons of Mahli, the son of Levi, the son of Israel, namely Sherebiah, and his sons and brothers, 18 men;

¹⁹ and Hashabiah and Jeshaiah of the sons of Merari, with his brothers and their sons, 20 men;

²⁰ and 220 of the temple servants, whom David and the princes had given for the service of the Levites, all of them designated by name.

²¹ Then I proclaimed a fast there at the river of Ahava, that we might humble ourselves before our God to seek from Him a safe journey for us, our little ones, and all our possessions.

²² For I was ashamed to request from the king troops and horsemen to protect us from the enemy on the way, because we had said to the king, "The hand of our God is favorably disposed to all those who seek Him, but His power and His

וָאֶשְׁלְחָה לֶאֱלִיעֶזֶר לַאֲרִיאֵל לִשְׁמַעְיָה ¹⁶
וּלְאֶלְנָתָן וּלְיָרִיב וּלְאֶלְנָתָן וּלְנָתָן וְלִזְכַרְיָה
וְלִמְשֻׁלָּם רָאשִׁים וּלְיוֹיָרִיב וּלְאֶלְנָתָן מְבִינִים׃
(וָאוֹצִאָה) [וָאֲצַוֶּה] אוֹתָם עַל־אִדּוֹ הָרֹאשׁ ¹⁷
בְּכָסִפְיָא הַמָּקוֹם וָאָשִׂימָה בְּפִיהֶם דְּבָרִים
לְדַבֵּר אֶל־אִדּוֹ אָחִיו (הַנְּתוּנִים) [הַנְּתִינִים]
בְּכָסִפְיָא הַמָּקוֹם לְהָבִיא־לָנוּ מְשָׁרְתִים לְבֵית
אֱלֹהֵינוּ׃
וַיָּבִיאוּ לָנוּ כְּיַד־אֱלֹהֵינוּ הַטּוֹבָה עָלֵינוּ אִישׁ ¹⁸
שֶׂכֶל מִבְּנֵי מַחְלִי בֶּן־לֵוִי בֶּן־יִשְׂרָאֵל וְשֵׁרֵבְיָה
וּבָנָיו וְאֶחָיו שְׁמֹנָה עָשָׂר׃
וְאֶת־חֲשַׁבְיָה וְאִתּוֹ יְשַׁעְיָה מִבְּנֵי מְרָרִי ¹⁹
אֶחָיו וּבְנֵיהֶם עֶשְׂרִים׃ ס
וּמִן־הַנְּתִינִים שֶׁנָּתַן דָּוִיד וְהַשָּׂרִים לַעֲבֹדַת ²⁰
הַלְוִיִּם נְתִינִים מָאתַיִם וְעֶשְׂרִים כֻּלָּם נִקְּבוּ
בְשֵׁמוֹת׃
וָאֶקְרָא שָׁם צוֹם עַל־הַנָּהָר אַהֲוָא ²¹
לְהִתְעַנּוֹת לִפְנֵי אֱלֹהֵינוּ לְבַקֵּשׁ מִמֶּנּוּ דֶּרֶךְ
יְשָׁרָה לָנוּ וּלְטַפֵּנוּ וּלְכָל־רְכוּשֵׁנוּ׃
כִּי בֹשְׁתִּי לִשְׁאוֹל מִן־הַמֶּלֶךְ חַיִל וּפָרָשִׁים ²²
לְעָזְרֵנוּ מֵאוֹיֵב בַּדָּרֶךְ כִּי־אָמַרְנוּ לַמֶּלֶךְ לֵאמֹר
יַד־אֱלֹהֵינוּ עַל־כָּל־מְבַקְשָׁיו לְטוֹבָה וְעֻזּוֹ וְאַפּוֹ
עַל כָּל־עֹזְבָיו׃
וַנָּצוּמָה וַנְּבַקְשָׁה מֵאֱלֹהֵינוּ עַל־זֹאת וַיֵּעָתֵר ²³
לָנוּ׃
וָאַבְדִּילָה מִשָּׂרֵי הַכֹּהֲנִים שְׁנֵים עָשָׂר ²⁴
לְשֵׁרֵבְיָה חֲשַׁבְיָה וְעִמָּהֶם מֵאֲחֵיהֶם עֲשָׂרָה׃
(וָאֶשְׁקוֹלָה) [וָאֶשְׁקֳלָה] לָהֶם אֶת־הַכֶּסֶף ²⁵
וְאֶת־הַזָּהָב וְאֶת־הַכֵּלִים תְּרוּמַת בֵּית־
אֱלֹהֵינוּ הַהֵרִימוּ הַמֶּלֶךְ וְיֹעֲצָיו וְשָׂרָיו וְכָל־
יִשְׂרָאֵל הַנִּמְצָאִים׃
וָאֶשְׁקֳלָה עַל־יָדָם כֶּסֶף כִּכָּרִים שֵׁשׁ־מֵאוֹת ²⁶
וַחֲמִשִּׁים וּכְלֵי־כֶסֶף מֵאָה לְכִכָּרִים זָהָב מֵאָה
כִכָּר׃
וּכְפֹרֵי זָהָב עֶשְׂרִים לַאֲדַרְכֹנִים אָלֶף וּכְלֵי ²⁷
נְחֹשֶׁת מֻצְהָב טוֹבָה שְׁנַיִם חֲמוּדֹת כַּזָּהָב׃
וָאֹמְרָה אֲלֵהֶם אַתֶּם קֹדֶשׁ לַיהוָה וְהַכֵּלִים ²⁸
קֹדֶשׁ וְהַכֶּסֶף וְהַזָּהָב נְדָבָה לַיהוָה אֱלֹהֵי
אֲבֹתֵיכֶם׃

anger are against all those who forsake Him."

23 So we fasted and sought our God concerning this *matter*, and He listened to our entreaty.

24 Then I set apart twelve of the leading priests, Sherebiah, Hashabiah, and with them ten of their brothers;

25 and I weighed out to them the silver, the gold and the utensils, the offering for the house of our God which the king and his counselors and his princes and all Israel present *there* had offered.

26 Thus I weighed into their hands 650 talents of silver, and silver utensils *worth* 100 talents, *and* 100 gold talents,

27 and 20 gold bowls *worth* 1,000 darics, and two utensils of fine shiny bronze, precious as gold.

28 Then I said to them, "You are holy to the LORD, and the utensils are holy; and the silver and the gold are a freewill offering to the LORD God of your fathers.

29 "Watch and keep *them* until you weigh *them* before the leading priests, the Levites and the heads of the fathers' *households* of Israel at Jerusalem, *in* the chambers of the house of the LORD."

30 So the priests and the Levites accepted the weighed out silver and gold and the utensils, to bring *them* to Jerusalem to the house of our God.

31 Then we journeyed from the river Ahava on the twelfth of the first month to go to Jerusalem; and the hand of our God was over us, and He delivered us from the hand of the enemy and the ambushes by the way.

29 שִׁקְדוּ וְשִׁמְרוּ עַד־תִּשְׁקְלוּ לִפְנֵי שָׂרֵי הַכֹּהֲנִים וְהַלְוִיִּם וְשָׂרֵי־הָאָבוֹת לְיִשְׂרָאֵל בִּירוּשָׁלִַם הַלְּשָׁכוֹת בֵּית יְהוָה:

30 וְקִבְּלוּ הַכֹּהֲנִים וְהַלְוִיִּם מִשְׁקַל הַכֶּסֶף וְהַזָּהָב וְהַכֵּלִים לְהָבִיא לִירוּשָׁלִַם לְבֵית אֱלֹהֵינוּ: פ

31 וַנִּסְעָה מִנְּהַר אַהֲוָא בִּשְׁנֵים עָשָׂר לַחֹדֶשׁ הָרִאשׁוֹן לָלֶכֶת יְרוּשָׁלִָם וְיַד־אֱלֹהֵינוּ הָיְתָה עָלֵינוּ וַיַּצִּילֵנוּ מִכַּף אוֹיֵב וְאוֹרֵב עַל־הַדָּרֶךְ:

32 וַנָּבוֹא יְרוּשָׁלִָם וַנֵּשֶׁב שָׁם יָמִים שְׁלֹשָׁה:

33 וּבַיּוֹם הָרְבִיעִי נִשְׁקַל הַכֶּסֶף וְהַזָּהָב וְהַכֵּלִים בְּבֵית אֱלֹהֵינוּ עַל יַד־מְרֵמוֹת בֶּן־אוּרִיָּה הַכֹּהֵן וְעִמּוֹ אֶלְעָזָר בֶּן־פִּינְחָס וְעִמָּהֶם יוֹזָבָד בֶּן־יֵשׁוּעַ וְנוֹעַדְיָה בֶן־בִּנּוּי הַלְוִיִּם:

34 בְּמִסְפָּר בְּמִשְׁקָל לַכֹּל וַיִּכָּתֵב כָּל־הַמִּשְׁקָל בָּעֵת הַהִיא: פ

35 הַבָּאִים מֵהַשְּׁבִי בְנֵי־הַגּוֹלָה הִקְרִיבוּ עֹלוֹת לֵאלֹהֵי יִשְׂרָאֵל פָּרִים שְׁנֵים־עָשָׂר עַל־כָּל־יִשְׂרָאֵל אֵילִים תִּשְׁעִים וְשִׁשָּׁה כְּבָשִׂים שִׁבְעִים וְשִׁבְעָה צְפִירֵי חַטָּאת שְׁנֵים עָשָׂר הַכֹּל עוֹלָה לַיהוָה: פ

36 וַיִּתְּנוּ אֶת־דָּתֵי הַמֶּלֶךְ לַאֲחַשְׁדַּרְפְּנֵי הַמֶּלֶךְ וּפַחֲווֹת עֵבֶר הַנָּהָר וְנִשְּׂאוּ אֶת־הָעָם וְאֶת־בֵּית־הָאֱלֹהִים: ס

[32] Thus we came to Jerusalem and remained there three days.

[33] On the fourth day the silver and the gold and the utensils were weighed out in the house of our God into the hand of Meremoth the son of Uriah the priest, and with him *was* Eleazar the son of Phinehas; and with them *were* the Levites, Jozabad the son of Jeshua and Noadiah the son of Binnui.

[34] Everything *was* numbered and weighed, and all the weight was recorded at that time.

[35] The exiles who had come from the captivity offered burnt offerings to the God of Israel: 12 bulls for all Israel, 96 rams, 77 lambs, 12 male goats for a sin offering, all as a burnt offering to the LORD.

[36] Then they delivered the king's edicts to the king's satraps and to the governors *in the provinces* beyond the River, and they supported the people and the house of God.

Process of Discovery

Linguistics Section

Linguistic Structure

[Head of Households who returned to Jerusalem] [1] Now these are the heads of their fathers' *households* and the genealogical enrollment of those who went up with me from Babylon in the reign of King Artaxerxes:

[2] of the sons of Phinehas, Gershom; of the sons of Ithamar, Daniel; of the sons of David, Hattush;

[3] of the sons of Shecaniah *who was* of the sons of Parosh, Zechariah and with him 150 males *who were in* the genealogical list;

[4] of the sons of Pahath-moab, Eliehoenai the son of Zerahiah and 200 males with him;

[5] of the sons of Zattu, Shecaniah, the son of Jahaziel and 300 males with him;

[6] and of the sons of Adin, Ebed the son of Jonathan and 50 males with him;

[7] and of the sons of Elam, Jeshaiah the son of Athaliah and 70 males with him;

[8] and of the sons of Shephatiah, Zebadiah the son of Michael and 80 males with him;

[9] of the sons of Joab, Obadiah the son of Jehiel and 218 males with him;

[10] and of the sons of Bani, Shelomith, the son of Josiphiah and 160 males with him;

[11] and of the sons of Bebai, Zechariah the son of Bebai and 28 males with him;

[12] and of the sons of Azgad, Johanan the son of Hakkatan and 110 males with him;

[13] and of the sons of Adonikam, the last ones, these being their names, Eliphelet, Jeuel and Shemaiah, and 60 males with them;

[14] and of the sons of Bigvai, Uthai and Zabbud, and 70 males with them.

[15] Now I assembled them at the river that runs to Ahava, where we camped for three days; and when I observed the people and the priests, I did not find any Levites there. [16] So I sent for Eliezer, Ariel, Shemaiah, Elnathan, Jarib, Elnathan, Nathan, Zechariah and Meshullam, leading men, and for Joiarib and Elnathan, teachers. [17] I sent them to Iddo the leading man at the place Casiphia; and I told them what to say to Iddo *and* his brothers, the temple servants at the place Casiphia, *that is*, to bring ministers to us for the house of our God. [18] According to the good hand of our God upon us they brought us a man of insight of the sons of Mahli, the son of Levi, the son of Israel, namely Sherebiah, and his sons and brothers, 18 men; [19] and Hashabiah and Jeshaiah of the sons of Merari, with his brothers and their sons, 20 men; [20] and 220 of the temple servants, whom David and the princes had given for the service of the Levites, all of them designated by name.

[21] Then I proclaimed a fast there at the river of Ahava, that we might humble ourselves before our God to seek from Him a safe journey for us, our little ones, and all our possessions. [22] For I was ashamed to request from the king troops and horsemen to

protect us from the enemy on the way, because we had said to the king, "The hand of our God is favorably disposed to all those who seek Him, but His power and His anger are against all those who forsake Him." [23] So we fasted and sought our God concerning this *matter*, and He listened to our entreaty.

[24] Then I set apart twelve of the leading priests, Sherebiah, Hashabiah, and with them ten of their brothers; [25] and I weighed out to them the silver, the gold and the utensils, the offering for the house of our God which the king and his counselors and his princes and all Israel present *there* had offered. [26] Thus I weighed into their hands 650 talents of silver, and silver utensils *worth* 100 talents, *and* 100 gold talents, [27] and 20 gold bowls *worth* 1,000 darics, and two utensils of fine shiny bronze, precious as gold.

[28] Then I said to them, "You are holy to the LORD, and the utensils are holy; and the silver and the gold are a freewill offering to the LORD God of your fathers. [29] "Watch and keep *them* until you weigh *them* before the leading priests, the Levites and the heads of the fathers' *households* of Israel at Jerusalem, *in* the chambers of the house of the LORD."

[30] So the priests and the Levites accepted the weighed out silver and gold and the utensils, to bring *them* to Jerusalem to the house of our God.

[31] Then we journeyed from the river Ahava on the twelfth of the first month to go to Jerusalem; and the hand of our God was over us, and He delivered us from the hand of the enemy and the ambushes by the way. [32] Thus we came to Jerusalem and remained there three days.

[33] On the fourth day the silver and the gold and the utensils were weighed out in the house of our God into the hand of Meremoth the son of Uriah the priest, and with him *was* Eleazar the son of Phinehas; and with them *were* the Levites, Jozabad the son of Jeshua and Noadiah the son of Binnui. [34] Everything *was* numbered and weighed, and all the weight was recorded at that time.

[35] The exiles who had come from the captivity offered burnt offerings to the God of Israel: 12 bulls for all Israel, 96 rams, 77 lambs, 12 male goats for a sin offering, all as a burnt offering to the LORD. [36] Then they delivered the king's edicts to the king's satraps and to the governors *in the provinces* beyond the River, and they supported the people and the house of God.

Discussion

This chapter lists the heads of the households who returned to Jerusalem. The middle of the chapter tells about the prayers of the people on their journey. The final third of the chapter describes the gifts that were given to the Temple.

Questioning the Passage

1. How much money is one daric? (v. 27)

The daric was a standard gold coin that was a currency in the Persian Empire.

Biblical Personalities

In this chapter, the people named were a part of the remnant who returned to Jerusalem for the rebuilding of the Temple.

Biblical Locations

1. Ahava[45]

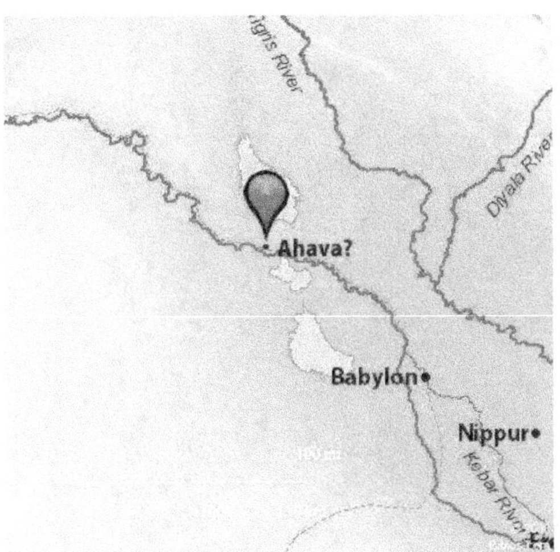

---

[45] Bible Map: Ahava, accessed January 29, 2021, https://bibleatlas.org/ahava.htm.

Thoughts

This chapter offers the names of the head of households who returned to Jerusalem. It also describes the financial costs involved with the reconstruction of the Temple.

Thoughts

Chapter Nine

Language

New American Standard 1995	Hebrew
[1] Now when these things had been completed, the princes approached me, saying, "The people of Israel and the priests and the Levites have not separated themselves from the peoples of the lands, according to their abominations, *those* of the Canaanites, the Hittites, the Perizzites, the Jebusites, the Ammonites, the Moabites, the Egyptians and the Amorites. [2] "For they have taken some of their daughters *as wives* for themselves and for their sons, so that the holy race has intermingled with the peoples of the lands; indeed, the hands of the princes and the rulers have been foremost in this unfaithfulness." [3] When I heard about this matter, I tore my garment and my robe, and pulled some of the hair from my head and my beard, and sat down appalled. [4] Then everyone who trembled at the words of the God of Israel on account of the unfaithfulness of the exiles gathered to me, and I sat appalled until the evening offering. [5] But at the evening offering I arose from my humiliation, even with my garment and my robe torn, and I fell on my knees and stretched out my hands to the LORD my God; [6] and I said, "O my God, I am ashamed and embarrassed to lift up my face to You, my God, for our iniquities have	וּכְכַלּוֹת אֵלֶּה נִגְּשׁוּ אֵלַי הַשָּׂרִים לֵאמֹר לֹא־נִבְדְּלוּ הָעָם יִשְׂרָאֵל וְהַכֹּהֲנִים וְהַלְוִיִּם מֵעַמֵּי הָאֲרָצוֹת כְּתוֹעֲבֹתֵיהֶם לַכְּנַעֲנִי הַחִתִּי הַפְּרִזִּי הַיְבוּסִי הָעַמֹּנִי הַמֹּאָבִי הַמִּצְרִי וְהָאֱמֹרִי: [2] כִּי־נָשְׂאוּ מִבְּנֹתֵיהֶם לָהֶם וְלִבְנֵיהֶם וְהִתְעָרְבוּ זֶרַע הַקֹּדֶשׁ בְּעַמֵּי הָאֲרָצוֹת וְיַד הַשָּׂרִים וְהַסְּגָנִים הָיְתָה בַּמַּעַל הַזֶּה רִאשׁוֹנָה: ס [3] וּכְשָׁמְעִי אֶת־הַדָּבָר הַזֶּה קָרַעְתִּי אֶת־בִּגְדִי וּמְעִילִי וָאֶמְרְטָה מִשְּׂעַר רֹאשִׁי וּזְקָנִי וָאֵשְׁבָה מְשׁוֹמֵם: [4] וְאֵלַי יֵאָסְפוּ כֹּל חָרֵד בְּדִבְרֵי אֱלֹהֵי־יִשְׂרָאֵל עַל מַעַל הַגּוֹלָה וַאֲנִי יֹשֵׁב מְשׁוֹמֵם עַד לְמִנְחַת הָעָרֶב: [5] וּבְמִנְחַת הָעֶרֶב קַמְתִּי מִתַּעֲנִיתִי וּבְקָרְעִי בִגְדִי וּמְעִילִי וָאֶכְרְעָה עַל־בִּרְכַּי וָאֶפְרְשָׂה כַפַּי אֶל־יְהוָה אֱלֹהָי: [6] וָאֹמְרָה אֱלֹהַי בֹּשְׁתִּי וְנִכְלַמְתִּי לְהָרִים אֱלֹהַי פָּנַי אֵלֶיךָ כִּי עֲוֹנֹתֵינוּ רָבוּ לְמַעְלָה רֹּאשׁ וְאַשְׁמָתֵנוּ גָדְלָה עַד לַשָּׁמָיִם: [7] מִימֵי אֲבֹתֵינוּ אֲנַחְנוּ בְּאַשְׁמָה גְדֹלָה עַד הַיּוֹם הַזֶּה וּבַעֲוֹנֹתֵינוּ נִתַּנּוּ אֲנַחְנוּ מְלָכֵינוּ כֹהֲנֵינוּ בְּיַד מַלְכֵי הָאֲרָצוֹת בַּחֶרֶב בַּשְּׁבִי וּבַבִּזָּה וּבְבֹשֶׁת פָּנִים כְּהַיּוֹם הַזֶּה: [8] וְעַתָּה כִּמְעַט־רֶגַע הָיְתָה תְחִנָּה מֵאֵת יְהוָה אֱלֹהֵינוּ לְהַשְׁאִיר לָנוּ פְּלֵיטָה וְלָתֶת־לָנוּ יָתֵד בִּמְקוֹם קָדְשׁוֹ

risen above our heads and our guilt has grown even to the heavens.

[7] "Since the days of our fathers to this day we *have been* in great guilt, and on account of our iniquities we, our kings *and* our priests have been given into the hand of the kings of the lands, to the sword, to captivity and to plunder and to open shame, as *it is* this day.

[8] "But now for a brief moment grace has been *shown* from the LORD our God, to leave us an escaped remnant and to give us a peg in His holy place, that our God may enlighten our eyes and grant us a little reviving in our bondage.

[9] "For we are slaves; yet in our bondage our God has not forsaken us, but has extended lovingkindness to us in the sight of the kings of Persia, to give us reviving to raise up the house of our God, to restore its ruins and to give us a wall in Judah and Jerusalem.

[10] "Now, our God, what shall we say after this? For we have forsaken Your commandments,

[11] which You have commanded by Your servants the prophets, saying, 'The land which you are entering to possess is an unclean land with the uncleanness of the peoples of the lands, with their abominations which have filled it from end to end *and* with their impurity.

[12] 'So now do not give your daughters to their sons nor take their daughters to your sons, and never seek their peace or their prosperity, that you may be strong and eat the good *things* of the land and leave *it* as an inheritance to your sons forever.'

[13] "After all that has come upon us for our evil deeds and our great guilt, since

לְהָאִיר עֵינֵינוּ אֱלֹהֵינוּ וּלְתִתֵּנוּ מִחְיָה מְעַט בְּעַבְדֻתֵנוּ:

[9] כִּי־עֲבָדִים אֲנַחְנוּ וּבְעַבְדֻתֵנוּ לֹא עֲזָבָנוּ אֱלֹהֵינוּ וַיַּט־עָלֵינוּ חֶסֶד לִפְנֵי מַלְכֵי פָרַס לָתֶת־לָנוּ מִחְיָה לְרוֹמֵם אֶת־בֵּית אֱלֹהֵינוּ וּלְהַעֲמִיד אֶת־חָרְבֹתָיו וְלָתֶת־לָנוּ גָדֵר בִּיהוּדָה וּבִירוּשָׁלָם: ס

[10] וְעַתָּה מַה־נֹּאמַר אֱלֹהֵינוּ אַחֲרֵי־זֹאת כִּי עָזַבְנוּ מִצְוֹתֶיךָ:

[11] אֲשֶׁר צִוִּיתָ בְּיַד עֲבָדֶיךָ הַנְּבִיאִים לֵאמֹר הָאָרֶץ אֲשֶׁר אַתֶּם בָּאִים לְרִשְׁתָּהּ אֶרֶץ נִדָּה הִיא בְּנִדַּת עַמֵּי הָאֲרָצוֹת בְּתוֹעֲבֹתֵיהֶם אֲשֶׁר מִלְאוּהָ מִפֶּה אֶל־פֶּה בְּטֻמְאָתָם:

[12] וְעַתָּה בְּנוֹתֵיכֶם אַל־תִּתְּנוּ לִבְנֵיהֶם וּבְנֹתֵיהֶם אַל־תִּשְׂאוּ לִבְנֵיכֶם וְלֹא־תִדְרְשׁוּ שְׁלֹמָם וְטוֹבָתָם עַד־עוֹלָם לְמַעַן תֶּחֶזְקוּ וַאֲכַלְתֶּם אֶת־טוּב הָאָרֶץ וְהוֹרַשְׁתֶּם לִבְנֵיכֶם עַד־עוֹלָם:

[13] וְאַחֲרֵי כָּל־הַבָּא עָלֵינוּ בְּמַעֲשֵׂינוּ הָרָעִים וּבְאַשְׁמָתֵנוּ הַגְּדֹלָה כִּי אַתָּה אֱלֹהֵינוּ חָשַׂכְתָּ לְמַטָּה מֵעֲוֹנֵנוּ וְנָתַתָּה לָנוּ פְּלֵיטָה כָּזֹאת:

[14] הֲנָשׁוּב לְהָפֵר מִצְוֹתֶיךָ וּלְהִתְחַתֵּן בְּעַמֵּי הַתֹּעֵבוֹת הָאֵלֶּה הֲלוֹא תֶאֱנַף־בָּנוּ עַד־כַּלֵּה לְאֵין שְׁאֵרִית וּפְלֵיטָה: פ

[15] יְהֹוָה אֱלֹהֵי יִשְׂרָאֵל צַדִּיק אַתָּה כִּי־נִשְׁאַרְנוּ פְלֵיטָה כְּהַיּוֹם הַזֶּה הִנְנוּ לְפָנֶיךָ בְּאַשְׁמָתֵינוּ כִּי אֵין לַעֲמוֹד לְפָנֶיךָ עַל־זֹאת: פ

You our God have requited *us* less than our iniquities *deserve*, and have given us an escaped remnant as this,

14 shall we again break Your commandments and intermarry with the peoples who commit these abominations? Would You not be angry with us to the point of destruction, until there is no remnant nor any who escape?

15 "O LORD God of Israel, You are righteous, for we have been left an escaped remnant, as *it is* this day; behold, we are before You in our guilt, for no one can stand before You because of this."

Process of Discovery

Linguistics Section

Linguistic Structure

[1] Now when these things had been completed, the princes approached me, saying, "The people of Israel and the priests and the Levites have not separated themselves from the peoples of the lands, according to their abominations, *those* of the Canaanites, the Hittites, the Perizzites, the Jebusites, the Ammonites, the Moabites, the Egyptians and the Amorites. [2] "For they have taken some of their daughters *as wives* for themselves and for their sons, so that the holy race has intermingled with the peoples of the lands; indeed, the hands of the princes and the rulers have been foremost in this unfaithfulness."

[3] When I heard about this matter, I tore my garment and my robe, and pulled some of the hair from my head and my beard, and sat down appalled. [4] Then everyone who trembled at the words of the God of Israel on account of the unfaithfulness of the exiles gathered to me, and I sat appalled until the evening offering. [5] But at the evening offering I arose from my humiliation, even with my garment and my robe torn, and I fell on my knees and stretched out my hands to the LORD my God; [6] and I said, "O my God, I am ashamed and embarrassed to lift up my face to You, my God, for our iniquities have risen above our heads and our guilt has grown even to the heavens. [7] "Since the days of our fathers to this day we *have been* in great guilt, and on account of our iniquities we, our kings *and* our priests have been given into the hand of the kings of the lands, to the sword, to captivity and to plunder and to open shame, as *it is* this day. [8] "But now for a brief moment grace has been *shown* from the LORD our God, to leave us an escaped remnant and to give us a peg in His holy place, that our God may enlighten our eyes and grant us a little reviving in our bondage. [9] "For we are slaves; yet in our bondage our God has not forsaken us, but has extended lovingkindness to us in the sight of the kings of Persia, to give us reviving to raise up the house of our God, to restore its ruins and to give us a wall in Judah and Jerusalem. [10] "Now, our God, what shall we say after this? For we have forsaken Your commandments, [11] which You have commanded by Your servants the prophets, saying, 'The land which you are entering to possess is an unclean land with the uncleanness of the peoples of the lands, with their abominations which have filled it from end to end *and* with their impurity. [12] 'So now do not give your daughters to their sons nor take their daughters to your sons, and never seek their peace or their prosperity, that you may be strong and eat the good *things* of the land and leave *it* as an inheritance to your sons forever.'

[13] "After all that has come upon us for our evil deeds and our great guilt, since You our God have requited *us* less than our iniquities *deserve*, and have given us an escaped remnant as this,

[14] shall we again break Your commandments and intermarry with the peoples who commit these abominations? Would You not be angry with us to the point of destruction, until there is no remnant nor any who escape?

[15] "O LORD God of Israel, You are righteous, for we have been left an escaped remnant, as *it is* this day; behold, we are before You in our guilt, for no one can stand before You because of this."

Discussion

Israel's problems with the peoples that occupied Judea are introduced, and Ezra prays to the LORD to forgive the people.

Questioning the Passage

1. What matters is verse one referring?

The matter was the reading and understanding of the King's letter that was sent to Ezra. Four months had passed since Ezra returned to Jerusalem. It was clear what the work was supposed to be.[46]

Thoughts

The LORD initiated the Exile to Babylon because the people had strayed from the Torah and the LORD's Word. The people had committed sins, and the worst was idolatry. Most of the corruption came from the peoples who lived in the land with the Israelites and the nations surrounding them. Ezra pleaded with the LORD because the people had finally returned from Exile and started to marry daughters of the pagan nations. The problem that was removed by the Exile had reappeared. How was Ezra going to stop the Israelites from sinning by taking on pagan spouses? Ezra said to the

---

[46] Nosson Scherman and Meir Zlotowitz, *The Writings = Kesuvim / The Writings: with a Commentary Anthologized from Rabbinic Writings = Ketuvim: 'im Perush Rashi, Metsudat Dayid, Metsudat Tsiyon, ye-'od* (Brooklyn, NY: Mesorah Publications, 2016).

LORD that he knew the people have sinned. How was this situation going to be corrected? That's the question at hand of this chapter.

Chapter Ten

Language

New American Standard 1995	Hebrew
[1] Now while Ezra was praying and making confession, weeping and prostrating himself before the house of God, a very large assembly, men, women and children, gathered to him from Israel; for the people wept bitterly. [2] Shecaniah the son of Jehiel, one of the sons of Elam, said to Ezra, "We have been unfaithful to our God and have married foreign women from the peoples of the land; yet now there is hope for Israel in spite of this. [3] "So now let us make a covenant with our God to put away all the wives and their children, according to the counsel of my lord and of those who tremble at the commandment of our God; and let it be done according to the law. [4] "Arise! For *this* matter is your responsibility, but we will be with you; be courageous and act." [5] Then Ezra rose and made the leading priests, the Levites and all Israel, take oath that they would do according to this proposal; so they took the oath. [6] Then Ezra rose from before the house of God and went into the chamber of Jehohanan the son of Eliashib. Although he went there, he did not eat bread nor drink water, for he was mourning over the unfaithfulness of the exiles. [7] They made a proclamation throughout Judah and Jerusalem to all the exiles, that they should assemble at Jerusalem,	וּכְהִתְפַּלֵּל עֶזְרָא וּכְהִתְוַדֹּתוֹ בֹּכֶה וּמִתְנַפֵּל לִפְנֵי בֵּית הָאֱלֹהִים נִקְבְּצוּ אֵלָיו מִיִּשְׂרָאֵל קָהָל רַב־מְאֹד אֲנָשִׁים וְנָשִׁים וִילָדִים כִּי־בָכוּ הָעָם הַרְבֵּה־בֶכֶה: ס [2] וַיַּעַן שְׁכַנְיָה בֶן־יְחִיאֵל מִבְּנֵי (עוֹלָם) [עֵילָם] וַיֹּאמֶר לְעֶזְרָא אֲנַחְנוּ מָעַלְנוּ בֵאלֹהֵינוּ וַנֹּשֶׁב נָשִׁים נָכְרִיּוֹת מֵעַמֵּי הָאָרֶץ וְעַתָּה יֵשׁ־מִקְוֶה לְיִשְׂרָאֵל עַל־זֹאת: [3] וְעַתָּה נִכְרָת־בְּרִית לֵאלֹהֵינוּ לְהוֹצִיא כָל־נָשִׁים וְהַנּוֹלָד מֵהֶם בַּעֲצַת אֲדֹנָי וְהַחֲרֵדִים בְּמִצְוַת אֱלֹהֵינוּ וְכַתּוֹרָה יֵעָשֶׂה: [4] קוּם כִּי־עָלֶיךָ הַדָּבָר וַאֲנַחְנוּ עִמָּךְ חֲזַק וַעֲשֵׂה: פ [5] וַיָּקָם עֶזְרָא וַיַּשְׁבַּע אֶת־שָׂרֵי הַכֹּהֲנִים הַלְוִיִּם וְכָל־יִשְׂרָאֵל לַעֲשׂוֹת כַּדָּבָר הַזֶּה וַיִּשָּׁבֵעוּ: [6] וַיָּקָם עֶזְרָא מִלִּפְנֵי בֵּית הָאֱלֹהִים וַיֵּלֶךְ אֶל־לִשְׁכַּת יְהוֹחָנָן בֶּן־אֶלְיָשִׁיב וַיֵּלֶךְ שָׁם לֶחֶם לֹא־אָכַל וּמַיִם לֹא־שָׁתָה כִּי מִתְאַבֵּל עַל־מַעַל הַגּוֹלָה: ס [7] וַיַּעֲבִירוּ קוֹל בִּיהוּדָה וִירוּשָׁלַם לְכֹל בְּנֵי הַגּוֹלָה לְהִקָּבֵץ יְרוּשָׁלָם: [8] וְכֹל אֲשֶׁר לֹא־יָבוֹא לִשְׁלֹשֶׁת הַיָּמִים כַּעֲצַת הַשָּׂרִים וְהַזְּקֵנִים יָחֳרַם כָּל־רְכוּשׁוֹ וְהוּא יִבָּדֵל מִקְּהַל הַגּוֹלָה: ס [9] וַיִּקָּבְצוּ כָל־אַנְשֵׁי־יְהוּדָה וּבִנְיָמִן יְרוּשָׁלַם לִשְׁלֹשֶׁת הַיָּמִים הוּא חֹדֶשׁ הַתְּשִׁיעִי בְּעֶשְׂרִים בַּחֹדֶשׁ וַיֵּשְׁבוּ כָל־הָעָם בִּרְחוֹב בֵּית הָאֱלֹהִים מַרְעִידִים עַל־הַדָּבָר וּמֵהַגְּשָׁמִים: פ [10] וַיָּקָם עֶזְרָא הַכֹּהֵן וַיֹּאמֶר אֲלֵהֶם אַתֶּם מְעַלְתֶּם וַתֹּשִׁיבוּ נָשִׁים נָכְרִיּוֹת לְהוֹסִיף עַל־אַשְׁמַת יִשְׂרָאֵל:

⁸ and that whoever would not come within three days, according to the counsel of the leaders and the elders, all his possessions should be forfeited and he himself excluded from the assembly of the exiles.

⁹ So all the men of Judah and Benjamin assembled at Jerusalem within the three days. It was the ninth month on the twentieth of the month, and all the people sat in the open square *before* the house of God, trembling because of this matter and the heavy rain.

¹⁰ Then Ezra the priest stood up and said to them, "You have been unfaithful and have married foreign wives adding to the guilt of Israel.

¹¹ "Now therefore, make confession to the LORD God of your fathers and do His will; and separate yourselves from the peoples of the land and from the foreign wives."

¹² Then all the assembly replied with a loud voice, "That's right! As you have said, so it is our duty to do.

¹³ "But there are many people; it is the rainy season and we are not able to stand in the open. Nor *can* the task *be done* in one or two days, for we have transgressed greatly in this matter.

¹⁴ "Let our leaders represent the whole assembly and let all those in our cities who have married foreign wives come at appointed times, together with the elders and judges of each city, until the fierce anger of our God on account of this matter is turned away from us."

¹⁵ Only Jonathan the son of Asahel and Jahzeiah the son of Tikvah opposed this,

וְעַתָּ֗ה תְּנ֥וּ תוֹדָ֛ה לַיהוָ֥ה אֱלֹהֵֽי־אֲבֹתֵיכֶ֖ם ¹¹ וַעֲשׂ֣וּ רְצוֹנ֑וֹ וְהִבָּדְלוּ֙ מֵעַמֵּ֣י הָאָ֔רֶץ וּמִן־הַנָּשִׁ֖ים הַנָּכְרִיּֽוֹת׃

וַיַּֽעֲנ֧וּ כָֽל־הַקָּהָ֛ל וַיֹּאמְר֖וּ ק֣וֹל גָּד֑וֹל כֵּ֛ן ¹² (כִּדְבָרֶ֖יךָ) [כִּדְבָרְךָ֛] עָלֵ֥ינוּ לַעֲשֽׂוֹת׃

אֲבָ֞ל הָעָ֥ם רָב֙ וְהָעֵ֣ת גְּשָׁמִ֔ים וְאֵ֥ין כֹּ֖חַ ¹³ לַעֲמ֣וֹד בַּח֑וּץ וְהַמְּלָאכָ֗ה לֹֽא־לְי֤וֹם אֶחָד֙ וְלֹ֣א לִשְׁנַ֔יִם כִּֽי־הִרְבִּ֥ינוּ לִפְשֹׁ֖עַ בַּדָּבָ֥ר הַזֶּֽה׃

יַעֲמְדוּ־נָ֣א שָׂרֵ֣ינוּ לְֽכָל־הַקָּהָ֗ל וְכֹ֣ל ׀ אֲשֶׁ֣ר ¹⁴ בֶּעָרֵ֡ינוּ הַהֹשִׁ֣יב נָשִׁ֣ים נָכְרִיּוֹת֩ יָבֹ֨א לְעִתִּ֜ים מְזֻמָּנִ֗ים וְעִמָּהֶ֛ם זִקְנֵי־עִ֥יר וָעִ֖יר וְשֹׁפְטֶ֑יהָ עַ֠ד לְהָשִׁ֞יב חֲר֤וֹן אַף־אֱלֹהֵ֙ינוּ֙ מִמֶּ֔נּוּ עַ֖ד לַדָּבָ֥ר הַזֶּֽה׃ פ

אַ֣ךְ יוֹנָתָ֧ן בֶּן־עֲשָׂהאֵ֛ל וְיַחְזְיָ֥ה בֶן־תִּקְוָ֖ה ¹⁵ עָמְד֣וּ עַל־זֹ֑את וּמְשֻׁלָּ֛ם וְשַׁבְּתַ֥י הַלֵּוִ֖י עֲזָרֻֽם׃

וַיַּֽעֲשׂוּ־כֵן֮ בְּנֵ֣י הַגּוֹלָה֒ וַיִּבָּדְלוּ֩ עֶזְרָ֨א הַכֹּהֵ֜ן ¹⁶ אֲנָשִׁ֗ים רָאשֵׁ֧י הָאָב֛וֹת לְבֵ֥ית אֲבֹתָ֖ם וְכֻלָּ֣ם בְּשֵׁמ֑וֹת וַיֵּשְׁב֗וּ בְּי֤וֹם אֶחָד֙ לַחֹ֣דֶשׁ הָעֲשִׂירִ֔י לְדַרְי֖וֹשׁ הַדָּבָֽר׃

וַיְכַלּ֣וּ בַכֹּ֔ל אֲנָשִׁ֕ים הַהֹשִׁ֖יבוּ נָשִׁ֣ים נָכְרִיּ֑וֹת ¹⁷ עַ֛ד י֥וֹם אֶחָ֖ד לַחֹ֥דֶשׁ הָרִאשֽׁוֹן׃ פ

וַיִּמָּצֵא֙ מִבְּנֵ֣י הַכֹּֽהֲנִ֔ים אֲשֶׁ֥ר הֹשִׁ֖יבוּ נָשִׁ֣ים ¹⁸ נָכְרִיּ֑וֹת מִבְּנֵ֨י יֵשׁ֤וּעַ בֶּן־יֽוֹצָדָק֙ וְאֶחָ֔יו מַעֲשֵׂיָה֙ וֶֽאֱלִיעֶ֔זֶר וְיָרִ֖יב וּגְדַלְיָֽה׃

וַיִּתְּנ֥וּ יָדָ֖ם לְהוֹצִ֣יא נְשֵׁיהֶ֑ם וַאֲשֵׁמִ֥ים אֵֽיל־ ¹⁹ צֹ֖אן עַל־אַשְׁמָתָֽם׃ ס

וּמִבְּנֵ֣י אִמֵּ֔ר חֲנָ֖נִי וּזְבַדְיָֽה׃ ס ²⁰

וּמִבְּנֵ֖י חָרִ֑ם מַעֲשֵׂיָ֤ה וְאֵֽלִיָּה֙ וּֽשְׁמַֽעְיָ֔ה ²¹ וִיחִיאֵ֖ל וְעֻזִּיָּֽה׃

וּמִבְּנֵ֖י פַּשְׁח֑וּר אֶלְיוֹעֵינַ֤י מַֽעֲשֵׂיָה֙ יִשְׁמָעֵ֔אל ²² נְתַנְאֵ֖ל יוֹזָבָ֥ד וְאֶלְעָשָֽׂה׃ ס

וּמִן־הַלְוִיִּ֖ם יוֹזָבָ֣ד וְשִׁמְעִ֑י וְקֵֽלָיָ֛ה ה֥וּא ²³ קְלִיטָ֖א פְּתַחְיָ֥ה יְהוּדָ֖ה וֶאֱלִיעֶֽזֶר׃ ס

וּמִן־הַמְשֹׁרְרִ֖ים אֶלְיָשִׁ֑יב וּמִן־הַשֹּׁעֲרִ֔ים ²⁴ שַׁלֻּ֥ם וָטֶ֖לֶם וְאוּרִֽי׃ ס

וּמִֽיִּשְׂרָאֵ֗ל מִבְּנֵ֣י פַרְעֹ֔שׁ רַמְיָ֥ה וְיִזִּיָּ֖ה ²⁵ וּמַלְכִּיָּ֛ה וּמִיָּמִ֥ן וְאֶלְעָזָ֖ר וּמַלְכִּיָּ֥ה וּבְנָיָֽה׃ ס

וּמִבְּנֵ֣י עֵילָ֔ם מַתַּנְיָ֥ה זְכַרְיָ֖ה וִיחִיאֵ֥ל וְעַבְדִּ֖י ²⁶ וִירֵמ֖וֹת וְאֵלִיָּֽה׃ ס

with Meshullam and Shabbethai the Levite supporting them.

¹⁶ But the exiles did so. And Ezra the priest selected men *who were* heads of fathers' *households* for *each of* their father's households, all of them by name. So they convened on the first day of the tenth month to investigate the matter.

¹⁷ They finished *investigating* all the men who had married foreign wives by the first day of the first month.

¹⁸ Among the sons of the priests who had married foreign wives were found of the sons of Jeshua the son of Jozadak, and his brothers: Maaseiah, Eliezer, Jarib and Gedaliah.

¹⁹ They pledged to put away their wives, and being guilty, *they offered* a ram of the flock for their offense.

²⁰ Of the sons of Immer *there were* Hanani and Zebadiah;

²¹ and of the sons of Harim: Maaseiah, Elijah, Shemaiah, Jehiel and Uzziah;

²² and of the sons of Pashhur: Elioenai, Maaseiah, Ishmael, Nethanel, Jozabad and Elasah.

²³ Of Levites *there were* Jozabad, Shimei, Kelaiah (that is, Kelita), Pethahiah, Judah and Eliezer.

²⁴ Of the singers *there was* Eliashib; and of the gatekeepers: Shallum, Telem and Uri.

²⁵ Of Israel, of the sons of Parosh *there were* Ramiah, Izziah, Malchijah, Mijamin, Eleazar, Malchijah and Benaiah;

²⁶ and of the sons of Elam: Mattaniah, Zechariah, Jehiel, Abdi, Jeremoth and Elijah;

²⁷ and of the sons of Zattu: Elioenai, Eliashib, Mattaniah, Jeremoth, Zabad and Aziza;

27 וּמִבְּנֵי זַתּוּא אֶלְיוֹעֵנַי אֶלְיָשִׁיב מַתַּנְיָה

וִירֵמוֹת וְזָבָד וַעֲזִיזָא: ס

28 וּמִבְּנֵי בֵּבָי יְהוֹחָנָן חֲנַנְיָה זַבַּי עַתְלָי: ס

29 וּמִבְּנֵי בָנִי מְשֻׁלָּם מַלּוּךְ וַעֲדָיָה יָשׁוּב וּשְׁאָל

(יְרֵמוֹת) [וְרָמוֹת]: ס

30 וּמִבְּנֵי פַּחַת מוֹאָב עַדְנָא וּכְלָל בְּנָיָה

מַעֲשֵׂיָה מַתַּנְיָה בְצַלְאֵל וּבִנּוּי וּמְנַשֶּׁה: ס

31 וּבְנֵי חָרִם אֱלִיעֶזֶר יִשִּׁיָּה מַלְכִּיָּה שְׁמַעְיָה

שִׁמְעוֹן:

32 בְּנְיָמִן מַלּוּךְ שְׁמַרְיָה: ס

33 מִבְּנֵי חָשֻׁם מַתְּנַי מַתַּתָּה זָבָד אֱלִיפֶלֶט

יְרֵמַי מְנַשֶּׁה שִׁמְעִי: ס

34 מִבְּנֵי בָנִי מַעֲדַי עַמְרָם וְאוּאֵל: ס

35 בְּנָיָה בֵדְיָה (כְּלֻהִי) [כְּלוּהוּ]:

36 וַנְיָה מְרֵמוֹת אֶלְיָשִׁיב:

37 מַתַּנְיָה מַתְּנַי (וְיַעֲשׂוֹ) [וְיַעֲשָׂי]:

38 וּבָנִי וּבִנּוּי שִׁמְעִי:

39 וְשֶׁלֶמְיָה וְנָתָן וַעֲדָיָה:

40 מַכְנַדְבַי שָׁשַׁי שָׁרָי:

41 עֲזַרְאֵל וְשֶׁלֶמְיָהוּ שְׁמַרְיָה:

42 שַׁלּוּם אֲמַרְיָה יוֹסֵף: ס

43 מִבְּנֵי נְבוֹ יְעִיאֵל מַתִּתְיָה זָבָד זְבִינָא (יַדּוֹ)

[יַדַּי] וְיוֹאֵל בְּנָיָה:

44 כָּל־אֵלֶּה (נָשְׂאֵי) [נָשְׂאוּ] נָשִׁים נָכְרִיּוֹת וְיֵשׁ

מֵהֶם נָשִׁים וַיָּשִׂימוּ בָּנִים: פ

[28] and of the sons of Bebai: Jehohanan, Hananiah, Zabbai *and* Athlai;

[29] and of the sons of Bani: Meshullam, Malluch and Adaiah, Jashub, Sheal *and* Jeremoth;

[30] and of the sons of Pahath-moab: Adna, Chelal, Benaiah, Maaseiah, Mattaniah, Bezalel, Binnui and Manasseh;

[31] and *of* the sons of Harim: Eliezer, Isshijah, Malchijah, Shemaiah, Shimeon,

[32] Benjamin, Malluch *and* Shemariah;

[33] of the sons of Hashum: Mattenai, Mattattah, Zabad, Eliphelet, Jeremai, Manasseh *and* Shimei;

[34] of the sons of Bani: Maadai, Amram, Uel,

[35] Benaiah, Bedeiah, Cheluhi,

[36] Vaniah, Meremoth, Eliashib,

[37] Mattaniah, Mattenai, Jaasu,

[38] Bani, Binnui, Shimei,

[39] Shelemiah, Nathan, Adaiah,

[40] Machnadebai, Shashai, Sharai,

[41] Azarel, Shelemiah, Shemariah,

[42] Shallum, Amariah *and* Joseph.

[43] Of the sons of Nebo *there were* Jeiel, Mattithiah, Zabad, Zebina, Jaddai, Joel *and* Benaiah.

[44] All these had married foreign wives, and some of them had wives *by whom* they had children.

Process of Discovery

Linguistics Section

Linguistic Structure

[Confessions] [1] Now while Ezra was praying and making confession, weeping and prostrating himself before the house of God, a very large assembly, men, women and children, gathered to him from Israel; for the people wept bitterly. [2] Shecaniah the son of Jehiel, one of the sons of Elam, said to Ezra, "We have been unfaithful to our God and have married foreign women from the peoples of the land; yet now there is hope for Israel in spite of this. [3] "So now let us make a covenant with our God to put away all the wives and their children, according to the counsel of my lord and of those who tremble at the commandment of our God; and let it be done according to the law. [4] "Arise! For *this* matter is your responsibility, but we will be with you; be courageous and act."

[Proclamation] [5] Then Ezra rose and made the leading priests, the Levites and all Israel, take oath that they would do according to this proposal; so they took the oath. [6] Then Ezra rose from before the house of God and went into the chamber of Jehohanan the son of Eliashib. Although he went there, he did not eat bread nor drink water, for he was mourning over the unfaithfulness of the exiles. [7] They made a proclamation throughout Judah and Jerusalem to all the exiles, that they should assemble at Jerusalem, [8] and that whoever would not come within three days, according to the counsel of the leaders and the elders, all his possessions should be forfeited and he himself excluded from the assembly of the exiles. [9] So all the men of Judah and Benjamin assembled at Jerusalem within the three days. It was the ninth month on the twentieth of the month, and all the people sat in the open square *before* the house of God, trembling because of this matter and the heavy rain.

[Proclamation] [10] Then Ezra the priest stood up and said to them, "You have been unfaithful and have married foreign wives adding to the guilt of Israel. [11] "Now therefore, make confession to the LORD God of your fathers and do His will; and separate yourselves from the peoples of the land and from the foreign wives." [12] Then all the assembly replied with a loud voice, "That's right! As you have said, so it is our duty to do.
[13] "But there are many people; it is the rainy season and we are not able to stand in the open. Nor *can* the task *be done* in one or two days, for we have transgressed greatly in this matter.

[Foreign wives list] [14] "Let our leaders represent the whole assembly and let all those in our cities who have married foreign wives come at appointed times, together with the elders and judges of each city, until the fierce anger of our God on account of this matter is turned away from us." [15] Only Jonathan the son of Asahel and Jahzeiah the son of Tikvah opposed this, with Meshullam and Shabbethai the Levite supporting them. [16] But the exiles did so. And Ezra the priest selected men *who were* heads of fathers' *households* for *each of* their father's households, all of them by name. So they convened on the first day of the tenth month to investigate the matter. [17] They finished *investigating* all the men who had married foreign wives by the first day of the first month. [18] Among the sons of the priests who had married foreign wives were found of the sons of Jeshua the son of Jozadak, and his brothers: Maaseiah, Eliezer, Jarib and Gedaliah. [19] They pledged to put away their wives, and being guilty, *they offered* a ram of the flock for their offense. [20] Of the sons of Immer *there were* Hanani and Zebadiah; [21] and of the sons of Harim: Maaseiah, Elijah, Shemaiah, Jehiel and Uzziah; [22] and of the sons of Pashhur: Elioenai, Maaseiah, Ishmael, Nethanel, Jozabad and Elasah. [23] Of Levites *there were* Jozabad, Shimei, Kelaiah (that is, Kelita), Pethahiah, Judah and Eliezer. [24] Of the singers *there was* Eliashib; and of the gatekeepers: Shallum, Telem and Uri. [25] Of Israel, of the sons of Parosh *there were* Ramiah, Izziah, Malchijah, Mijamin, Eleazar, Malchijah and Benaiah; [26] and of the sons of Elam: Mattaniah, Zechariah, Jehiel, Abdi, Jeremoth and Elijah; [27] and of the sons of Zattu: Elioenai, Eliashib, Mattaniah, Jeremoth, Zabad and Aziza; [28] and of the sons of Bebai: Jehohanan, Hananiah, Zabbai *and* Athlai; [29] and of the sons of Bani: Meshullam, Malluch and Adaiah, Jashub, Sheal *and* Jeremoth; [30] and of the sons of Pahath-moab: Adna, Chelal, Benaiah, Maaseiah, Mattaniah, Bezalel, Binnui and Manasseh; [31] and *of* the sons of Harim: Eliezer, Isshijah, Malchijah, Shemaiah, Shimeon, [32] Benjamin, Malluch *and* Shemariah; [33] of the sons of Hashum: Mattenai, Mattattah, Zabad, Eliphelet, Jeremai, Manasseh *and* Shimei; [34] of the sons of Bani: Maadai, Amram, Uel, [35] Benaiah, Bedeiah, Cheluhi, [36] Vaniah, Meremoth, Eliashib, [37] Mattaniah, Mattenai, Jaasu, [38] Bani, Binnui, Shimei, [39] Shelemiah, Nathan, Adaiah, [40] Machnadebai, Shashai, Sharai, [41] Azarel, Shelemiah, Shemariah, [42] Shallum, Amariah *and* Joseph. [43] Of the sons of Nebo *there were* Jeiel, Mattithiah, Zabad, Zebina, Jaddai, Joel *and* Benaiah. [44] All these had married foreign wives, and some of them had wives *by whom* they had children.

Discussion

This chapter is a continuation from chapter nine, dealing with the men who returned to Jerusalem and married Gentile women. Ezra and the assembly of elders decided what they needed to do. A list of the men and their sons is offered.

Thoughts

In Ezra's day, it was believed that it was a sin to marry outside of the Hebrew race. It was difficult for the men who married outside the race to have to abandon their families. The list may have been to indicate who had done this. The purity of nations and races was a strong belief in ancient times. In several areas of today's world, this is still true. The idea of racial purity was a source of genocide and war. It is a sad attribute of humanity.

Bibliography

Abarim Publications. "The Amazing Name Bishlam: Meaning and Etymology." Abarim Publications. Abarim Publications. Accessed January 22, 2021. https://www.abarim-publications.com/Meaning/Bishlam.html.

"Artaxerxes I." Encyclopædia Britannica. Encyclopædia Britannica, inc. Accessed January 22, 2021. https://www.britannica.com/biography/Artaxerxes-I.

"Babylonia." Wikipedia. Wikimedia Foundation, January 22, 2021. https://en.wikipedia.org/wiki/Babylonia.

Bergstein, Avrohom. "Nebuchadnezzar The Evil Babylonian King Who Destroyed Jerusalem." Chabad. Accessed January 25, 2021. https://www.chabad.org/library/article_cdo/aid/4451665/jewish/Nebuchadnezzar.htm.

Bible Map: Ahava. Accessed January 29, 2021. https://bibleatlas.org/ahava.htm.

"Cyrus the Great." Encyclopædia Britannica. Encyclopædia Britannica, inc. Accessed January 9, 2021. https://www.britannica.com/biography/Cyrus-the-great.

Denova, Rebecca. "Jerusalem." Ancient History Encyclopedia. Ancient History Encyclopedia, January 9, 2021. https://www.ancient.eu/jerusalem/.

"Erech." Encyclopædia Britannica. Encyclopædia Britannica, inc. Accessed January 22, 2021. https://www.britannica.com/place/Erech.

Errico, Rocco A., and George M. Lamsa. *Aramaic Light on Ezra through the Song of Solomon*. Smyma, GA: Noohra Foundation, 2010.

GotQuestions.org. "Home." GotQuestions.org, August 13, 2018.
https://www.gotquestions.org/Sheshbazzar-in-the-Bible.html.

History of Iran: Elamite Empire. Accessed January 22, 2021.
http://www.iranchamber.com/history/elamite/elamite.php.

"JewishEncyclopedia.com." AHASUERUS - JewishEncyclopedia.com. Accessed
January 22, 2021. http://www.jewishencyclopedia.com/articles/967-ahasuerus.

"Judah." Encyclopædia Britannica. Encyclopædia Britannica, inc. Accessed January
13, 2021. https://www.britannica.com/topic/Judah-Hebrew-tribe.

Mark, Joshua J. "Esarhaddon." Ancient History Encyclopedia. Ancient History
Encyclopedia, January 11, 2021. https://www.ancient.eu/Esarhaddon/.

Nappa, Mike. "Who Was Zerubbabel in the Bible?" Christianity.com. Salem Web
Network, July 24, 2019. https://www.christianity.com/wiki/people/who-was-
zerubbabel-in-the-bible.html.

"Nethinim Definition and Meaning - Bible Dictionary." biblestudytools.com.
Accessed January 29, 2021.
https://www.biblestudytools.com/dictionary/nethinim/.

Osnappar - Encyclopedia of The Bible - Bible Gateway. Accessed January 22, 2021.
https://www.biblegateway.com/resources/encyclopedia-of-the-bible/Osnappar.

Posner, Menachem. What is Sukkot? Accessed January 18, 2021.
https://www.chabad.org/library/article_cdo/aid/4784/jewish/What-Is-
Sukkot.htm.

"Rehum Definition and Meaning - Bible Dictionary." biblestudytools.com. Accessed January 22, 2021. https://www.biblestudytools.com/dictionary/rehum/.

Rosenberg, A. J. *Daniel, Ezra, Nehemiah: a New English Translation = Sifrê Dāniyyel, 'Ezrâ, Neḥemyā.* New York: Judaica Pr., 1991.

Scherman, Nosson, and Meir Zlotowitz. *The Writings = Kesuvim / The Writings: with a Commentary Anthologized from Rabbinic Writings = Ketuvim: 'im Perush Rashi, Metsudat David, Metsudat Tsiyon, ve-'od.* Brooklyn, NY: Mesorah Publications, 2016.

Shethar-Bozenai - Encyclopedia of The Bible - Bible Gateway. Accessed January 25, 2021. https://www.biblegateway.com/resources/encyclopedia-of-the-bible/Shethar-Bozenai.

"Shimshai Definition and Meaning - Bible Dictionary." biblestudytools.com. Accessed January 22, 2021. https://www.biblestudytools.com/dictionary/shimshai/.

Staff, BibleStudyTools. "Book of Haggai - Read, Study Bible Verses Online." biblestudytools.com. BibleStudyTools, January 25, 2021. https://www.biblestudytools.com/haggai/.

Study.com. Accessed January 13, 2021. https://study.com/academy/answer/who-is-jeshua-in-the-book-of-ezra.html.

"Susa." Encyclopædia Britannica. Encyclopædia Britannica, inc. Accessed January 22, 2021. https://www.britannica.com/place/Susa.

"Tabeel Definition and Meaning - Bible Dictionary." biblestudytools.com. Accessed January 22, 2021. https://www.biblestudytools.com/dictionary/tabeel/.

"Tattenai." Encyclopædia Britannica. Encyclopædia Britannica, inc. Accessed January 25, 2021. https://www.britannica.com/biography/Tattenai.

Topical Bible: Asaph. Accessed January 22, 2021. https://biblehub.com/topical/a/asaph.htm.

Topical Bible: Henadad. Accessed January 22, 2021. https://biblehub.com/topical/h/henadad.htm.

Topical Bible: Kadmiel. Accessed January 22, 2021. https://biblehub.com/topical/k/kadmiel.htm.

Topical Bible: Mithredath. Accessed January 22, 2021. https://biblehub.com/topical/m/mithredath.htm.

"Trans-Euphrates." WordPanda. Accessed January 22, 2021. https://wordpanda.net/definition/trans-euphrates.

"The Tribe of Benjamin." israel. Accessed January 13, 2021. https://www.israel-a-history-of.com/tribe-of-benjamin.html.

Williamson, H. G. M. *Word Biblical Commentary*. 16. Vol. 16. Waco, TX: Word Books, 1985.

Zavada, Jack. "Ancient Samaria: Find Out How Jesus Approached Racism in His Day." Learn Religions. Accessed January 22, 2021. https://www.learnreligions.com/history-of-samaria-4062174.

END NOTES

[i] "Levi ben Gershon (Ralbag) was a Provencal philosopher, physician, mathematician, astronomer, Talmudic commentator and Torah commentator. He seems to never have accepted a rabbinic post, and little is known about his life – even the place and date of his death is unclear. Ralbag was a strict Aristotelian, and in his great philosophical work, Milchamot Hashem, he critiques Rambam on some points where he deviates from Aristotelian teaching. He was also a fervent believer in astrology, and astrological determinism pervades his philosophical work, though he did maintain the notion of human free-will. His philosophical views lead to opposition to his works in some circles. His mathematical works were sophisticated, influential and ground-breaking; he is noted for his work in combinatorics and early use of the principle of mathematical induction. Some of these works were even translated into Latin at the request of Christian scholars. The Ralbag was credited for inventing the 'Jacob's staff,' an astronomical device. Finally, he is perhaps best known today for his commentary on the Tanach, which displays his wide learning and interweaves halachic matters and rulings. He wrote several Talmudic works, most of which have since been lost." https://www.sefaria.org/person/Ralbag

[ii] "Rashi was the outstanding Biblical commentator of the Middle Ages. He was born in Troyes, France, and lived from 1040 to 1105, surviving the massacres of the First Crusade through Europe. His father Yitzchak was a great scholar, but very poor, making his living from the sale of wine." Source: https://www.jewishvirtuallibrary.org/rabbi-shlomo-yitzchaki-rashi